T0208523

Heaven, Hell, *and* *Other* Bible Controversies

- Eyewitness Reports of Heaven and Hell?
- Is Hell Really an Eternal Fire?
- Do the Dead Get a Second Chance to Go to Heaven?
- Pre-existence and Reincarnation—Are They Biblical?
- Melchizedek and Jesus—Two of Many Divine Incarnations?

JACOB GREMIEL

authorHOUSE®

AuthorHouse™
1663 Liberty Drive
Bloomington, IN 47403
www.authorhouse.com
Phone: 833-262-8899

© 2021 Jacob Gremiel. All rights reserved.

No part of this book may be reproduced, stored in a retrieval system, or transmitted by any means without the written permission of the author.

Published by AuthorHouse   03/17/2022

ISBN: 978-1-6655-4450-4 (sc)
ISBN: 978-1-6655-4448-1 (hc)
ISBN: 978-1-6655-4449-8 (e)

Library of Congress Control Number: 2021923397

Print information available on the last page.

Any people depicted in stock imagery provided by Getty Images are models, and such images are being used for illustrative purposes only. Certain stock imagery © Getty Images.

This book is printed on acid-free paper.

Because of the dynamic nature of the Internet, any web addresses or links contained in this book may have changed since publication and may no longer be valid. The views expressed in this work are solely those of the author and do not necessarily reflect the views of the publisher, and the publisher hereby disclaims any responsibility for them.

Scripture quotations marked NIV are taken from the Holy Bible, New International Version®. NIV®. Copyright © 1973, 1978, 1984 by International Bible Society. Used by permission of Zondervan. All rights reserved. [Biblica]

Scripture quotations marked NKJV are taken from the New King James Version. Copyright © 1982 by Thomas Nelson, Inc. Used by permission. All rights reserved.

CONTENTS

PART III
Other Questions about Heaven and Hell

PART IV
Other Questions about Christianity

INTRODUCTION

I would wager that anyone who reads this book knows at least some of the basic Biblical facts relating to Heaven and Hell. We all know, for example, that what we do in this life factors in to whether we go to Heaven or Hell. We also know that Heaven is considered the destination we strive to reach and Hell the one we strive to avoid.

However, as I've learned from countless discussions on this topic, many of us scratch our heads over a number of things that we don't know about Heaven and Hell: Does the Bible clearly say that Heaven and Hell are real destinations for us after we die? Is there any proof of Heaven and Hell outside of the Bible? Are people who have never heard of Jesus doomed to Hell? Can people of other religions go to Heaven?

I would also wager that most of us have at least briefly wondered about other even more controversial topics that are directly and indirectly related to Heaven and Hell: Do we get a second chance to receive salvation after we die? Is Hell really eternal fire? Do our souls exist before we are born? Is there a spiritual connection between Jesus Christ and Melchizedek?

Fortunately, we have answers for these and many more hitherto unanswered questions and controversies, and all of our answers will be based on clear Biblical teachings. As a bonus, we will see strong evidence outside of the Bible that Heaven and Hell are as real as our earthly planet or the homes that we live in. What kind of evidence is this? Clearly the strongest kind possible—recent eyewitness accounts from people who have actually gone to both places and returned to tell about them!

So let's buckle up and prepare ourselves for a unique, enlightening, and extremely interesting ride through less traveled paths of questions, answers, discussions, and controversies about Heaven, Hell, and other still-debated Bible topics.

PART I

Heaven and Hell in the Bible

CHAPTER I

Does the Bible Really Say That Heaven and Hell Exist?

Before we discuss the existence of Heaven and Hell, let's make sure we're on the same page about what they are. The Bible tells us generally that Heaven is a beautiful place where souls deemed worthy enough will experience eternal life, peace, love, joy, and righteousness in God's presence.

Hell is the opposite. It is an ugly place where souls deemed evil and unworthy of Heaven will experience "eternal death" (more about this later) and have a very unpleasant existence outside of God's presence.

Regarding the existence of Heaven and Hell, I can't help but smile at skeptics who insist that verses that make reference to both places are simply part of elaborate allegories functioning as our moral compasses. My answer to these skeptics? Utter nonsense! But let's not just take my word for it; the Bible can speak for itself, loudly and clearly:

Verses Confirming the Reality of Heaven

2 Corinthians 5:1:

For we know that if the earthly tent we live in is destroyed, we have a building from God, an eternal house in Heaven, not built by human hands. (NIV)

This verse refers to two real places, one on earth and the other in Heaven, and tells us unequivocally that we have homes in both.

Philippians 3:20 (NIV)

But our citizenship is in Heaven. And we eagerly await a Savior from there, the Lord Jesus Christ, who, by the power that enables him to bring everything under his control, will transform our lowly bodies so that they will be like his glorious body.

The Bible talks not only about the reality of Heaven, but also about the non-physical bodies that we will need for our non-physical existence there.

Heaven Confirmed

These are just two of the many verses that tell us of the real existence of Heaven. As an added bonus, we even have Biblical reports from people who personally witnessed Heaven for themselves:

Biblical Eyewitnesses of Heaven

Revelation 21:10

And he carried me away in the Spirit to a mountain great and high, and showed me the Holy City, Jerusalem, coming down out of heaven from God. (NIV)

John's experience sounds very much like what we would now call a near-death experience (NDE) of heaven, as he specifies that he was "in the Spirit." I've heard some naysayers' claim that John was just having a vision. However, they either fail to realize or they ignore the fact that the relevant Greek word used here--πνεύματι (pronounced 'pneumati')--means spirit, not vision. There are Greek words for vision, a common one being όραμα (pronounced 'orama'), but none of those words is πνεύματι.

2 Corinthians 12: 2-4 (NIV)

I know a man in Christ who fourteen years ago was caught up to the third heaven. Whether it was in the body or out of the body I do not know—God knows.

And I know that this man—whether in the body or apart from the body I do not know, but God knows— was caught up to paradise and heard inexpressible things, things that no one is permitted to tell.

This is Paul's description of his out-of-body journey to a place he first called "the third heaven." Saying he didn't know whether he was in or out of his body at the time is a strong indication of how real the trip was to him. Obviously his awareness during the trip was just as clear, if not more so, as it would have been in his physical body.

We know that it was Paul who took this trip, although he doesn't actually name himself, being reluctant to exalt himself by doing so.

Third Heaven?

Again, Paul doesn't just say he went to Heaven, but rather "to the third heaven," from the Greek ἕως τρίτου οὐρανοῦ (heos tritou ouranou). He also refers to the place he went to as *Paradise*, from the Greek παράδεισος (parádeisos) -- a place where he says he learned profound things that people on earth were not permitted to know.

We'll discuss Paul's heavenly trip as well as the terms 'Heaven' and 'Paradise' in more detail a little later.

What about Hell?

Okay, now that we're sure that the Bible teaches that Heaven is a real place, what about Hell? Does the Bible confirm that too? Absolutely! Here are two of the many verses that do just that:

Verses Confirming the Reality of Hell

1 Thessalonians 1:9 (NIV)

They will be punished with everlasting destruction and shut out from the presence of the Lord and from the glory of his might.

Matthew 8:12 (NIV)

But the subjects of the kingdom will be thrown outside, into the darkness, where there will be weeping and gnashing of teeth.

These verses show the characteristic marks of Hell—unpleasantness and separation from God.

Evidence of Heaven and Hell Outside of the Bible?

These were just a tiny fraction of the total verses on Heaven and Hell, but I'm sure they more than suffice in delivering their unmistakable message that Heaven and Hell are real. The question now is whether we have any evidence outside of the Bible to corroborate this Biblical message. The answer, of course, is yes! In the next few chapters we will review the experiences of ordinary modern people like you and I who have seen Heaven and Hell and lived to tell about them.

PART II

Modern People Who Have Recently Witnessed Heaven and Hell

CHAPTER II

The Evangelist Who Died Three Times and Reluctantly Returned From Heaven

As much as I'm amused at skeptics who insist that the Bible does not really say that Heaven and Hell are real, I'm even more tickled when they assert that there is no proof of Heaven and Hell and no life after death.

Well, I have interviewed dozens of people who represent living proof of Heaven and Hell because they saw both places for themselves during what are often called near-death experiences (NDEs) And some of these people were declared clinically dead at the time. By the way, correct me if I'm wrong, but if we consciously experience Heaven and Hell *after* doctors declare us dead, doesn't that also mean that there is an afterlife? Just checking.

Without further ado, let's review and discuss perhaps the most astounding and inspirational case of a person dying, going to Heaven, and returning to talk about it that I've ever read or heard of:

A Philadelphia Evangelist

Mr. Melvin was a very popular African American evangelist in his sixties who had preached for decades, mostly in the Philadelphia area.

Nobody could ignite a spiritual blaze throughout the congregation like Mr. Melvin. If you were tired or bored before he started preaching, you wouldn't be that way after he got warmed up. If you didn't shout 'amen!,' bounce in your pew, or dance in the aisles at least once during his sermons, it meant that you somehow couldn't hear him or were seriously ill.

Being an evangelist, he traveled to different churches in different states, but spent most of his time in the Philadelphia area where, without a doubt, Mr. Melvin was a spiritual treat for his congregations.

Parallels or Coincidences?

God also used Mr. Melvin to heal others through the laying on of hands. Invariably after his sermons, he would invite the congregation to come forward for healing prayer, and numerous people were delivered from whatever was afflicting them.

As I'm sure most of us know, however, people used by God to heal others sometimes need healing themselves. And so it was with Mr. Melvin. He was chronically ill for years, due to a bad heart and other physical problems, yet God used him to heal others. This fact and a number of others made me think of interesting things that Mr. Melvin seemed to have in common with the Apostle Paul:

First, like Paul, Mr. Melvin healed others but was physically afflicted himself. Both men seemed to have what Paul called "a thorn in the flesh" that was perhaps there to keep him humble. (2 Corinthians 12:7 NIV):

"...Therefore, in order to keep me from becoming conceited, I was given a thorn in my flesh,..."

Another parallel was that they were both still very much on fire for God until the very end of their life on earth.

A third parallel, and certainly the most amazing, was that that they both witnessed Heaven and returned to earth to tell about it.

Do these parallels mean anything? Well, no one can be sure. Perhaps they just mean that God used these two men and others as special messengers to deliver the simple message that Heaven is real. Here are the details of Mr. Melvin's amazing experiences with Heaven:

He Suffered a Severe Stroke at Home

On the day of his first trip to Heaven, Mr. Melvin suffered a severe stroke while home alone. His wife was away, but fortunately, his daughter, who lived with them, returned home from work and discovered him unconscious but still breathing on the living room floor. She called the ambulance and they rushed him to the emergency ward where they began treating him immediately.

The Doctors Pronounced Him Dead

"I woke up and knew I was on the operating table, because I could hear the doctors talking. I was confused and afraid, because I couldn't move and couldn't open my eyes to see anything. Then I heard the doctors saying my vital signs were failing and they were losing me. Then they said I was gone. One of them shouted orders to try to restart my heart. Then it really hit me what was happening to me. They said I was dead and were trying to revive me."

He Left His Dead Body and Saw Everything That Was Happening

"All of a sudden I felt myself rising upwards from the operating table towards the ceiling. It was a strange floating flying kind of feeling. I knew almost immediately that I was in the spirit, because I could now move and see and could see my body laying there on the table. I was just kind of hovering there in mid-air and I could see and hear everything and everyone in the room, including the doctors. I could hear them running around yelling that my vital signs had stopped and trying to bring that body back to life. But they couldn't.

"I was part fascinated and part amused by everything that was happening, and I wanted to tell them to stop working on that old sick shell on the table, because it wasn't really me. The real me was up here near the ceiling. And the real me, thank God, was finally feeling no pain. I was finally free from my suffering."

He Flew Through a Tunnel and Encountered Angels

"Then suddenly, as I was still watching them working on that body, I felt myself being pulled away and found myself flying through what looked like a kind of a tunnel. It was dark inside, and I was flying toward a light at the other end of it.

When I got to the end, there were some beings there to greet me. They were beautiful radiant beings that had to be angels. I believe they were my guardian angels, because I felt safe and protected in their presence. I had no fear at all.

Angels Escorted Him to Paradise

"They took me to a place that I just knew was Heaven. I had no doubt at all. It was a real paradise. It was so beautiful, I don't think any of our languages on earth could really describe it. I can try to describe some of the things I saw and heard. I saw clear, sparkling water with bright lights reflecting off of it. I saw pastures with bright beautiful shades of green. As a matter of fact there were beautiful colors all around, everywhere. And, oh my, the music. The music was all around me too, and as beautiful as the colors, or maybe even more so. It was soft and soothing and peaceful. It was like a heavenly countryside outside of a heavenly city. The entire place was just filled with beauty and peace. And believe it or not, it got even better than that."

He Stood Before Jesus Christ

"Suddenly I was in the presence of a being that seemed to be made of very bright light. I knew it was Jesus Christ Himself. No doubt at all. He didn't say it, and I didn't have to guess either. I just knew it.

Jesus Radiated Pure Love

"And that light that radiated out of Jesus felt like pure love. Purer and stronger than I could ever have imagined. The closest thing I can compare it with is the kind of love that I would sometimes feel when I was alone in prayer and the Lord's spirit would sort of overflow inside me. I used to call that pure love.

But the love I felt standing there in His presence in Heaven was 100 times purer and stronger. I was overwhelmed by His love and the joy that it gave me, and I just knew that I wanted to spend eternity there with Him. I certainly did not want to go back to that sick body on earth. As soon as that thought crossed my mind, He told me I had to go back."

He Had to Return to Earth

"I begged and begged Jesus to let me stay, but He explained to me in my mind that I had to go back because there were things on earth that I still needed to do. I was devastated at first, but I felt a little better when He told me that my work on earth would be done very soon and that I would be coming back to Him right afterwards.

"Then He showed me a kind of window where I could see my body in the hospital and a group of people standing around it and praying for me to be revived. They were relatives and people from the churches where I preached, including some of you all. I recognized everybody. He made me understand that your prayers were part of the reason I was going back.

"It felt like I was being pulled back into my body by some strong but gentle force. And suddenly there I was in my body again. I opened my eyes and looked around, and the first thing I saw was the same group of people that I saw from Heaven. And the first thing I heard was them praising God for working a miracle and resurrecting me from the dead."

The Doctors Were Stunned by His Recovery

"Even the doctors called it a miracle that I came back. They told me they had no idea how or why I was alive and admitted that it must have been something beyond their knowledge or abilities. They kept me in the hospital for several more days, feeding me through tubes and running tests.

And almost every time they talked to me, they would ask me about my experiences on the other side. And they would look at me and listen in amazement as I repeated this part or that part of the story. I must have told them a dozen times, but each time the wonder on their faces made it seem like it was the first time they had heard it."

He Returned to His Ministry

After a few days of recovery and relaxation, Mr. Melvin returned home and then eventually to the pulpit where he resumed his sermons and told of his experiences in Heaven. But he had changed in certain ways, and everyone noticed it. In addition to having a stronger sense of purpose about his witnessing for God and a more fearless attitude toward life, he showed more love, tolerance, and forgiveness toward everyone. And perhaps even more noticeable was the fact that more people seemed to be healed during his post-sermon laying on of hands.

"Please Don't Pray for Me Next Time I Die"

Every once in a while after his stories about his trip to Heaven, he would tell his congregations in a lighthearted way, "Please don't pray for me the next time I die." The people thought he was kidding, but inside he was actually serious about it. But he kept it wrapped in a humorous tone so that no one would take it the wrong way.

Although a big part of his remaining mission on earth was spreading the good news about the reality of God and Heaven, he knew God did not want him to dampen anyone's enthusiasm for doing God's work on earth. So he made it a point to add to some of his sermons: "Remember, saints, God is as real on earth as He is in Heaven."

Another reason why Mr. Melvin was lighthearted about not wanting the people to pray for him during his next trip to Heaven was that he was convinced that the Lord would allow him to stay the next time, despite any prayers that went up. In addition, his stronger sense of purpose and fearlessness led him to not only continue his ministry, but, against the recommendations of his doctors and the wishes of some of his loved ones, he actually increased it.

He wanted to be found doing the will of the Lord every minute that he could, because, as he would often say during his sermons, "I know I'm soon going to spend eternity in Paradise."

But Mr. Melvin's eternal stay in Heaven was delayed a little longer than he anticipated.

Mr. Melvin's Second Trip to Heaven

In a few short weeks after increasing his work load, Mr. Melvin suffered more physical complications, was again pronounced dead by the doctors, and took another trip to Heaven that was nearly identical to the first one. And again, his lifeless body was surrounded by church members and relatives who, again, prayed for his return to earth. And sure enough, to his disappointment, he again returned.

His Second Return to the Pulpit

After several days of recuperation, he predictably returned to the pulpit: "It was very much like the first time, saints, only better," he said, scanning the congregation with a slight smile. He was right. His description of his second trip to Heaven sounded nearly identical to the first one, except this time he talked about the astounding scenery and the love and majesty of Jesus as one who had seen them before and was ecstatic to see again.

Then, he commented about returning to earth a second time: "Listen, saints," he started. I really thank you for the love you've showed me and for your prayers and faith that brought me back once again." He paused, apparently searching for the right words. "I hope you don't take this the wrong way, because I love you all and I love being here with you. But to be perfectly honest, I would really rather be in Heaven with Jesus right now, wouldn't you?" he smiled widely, drawing a chorus of 'amens' around the church.

"Please Don't Pray for Me Next Time I Die"

"I know that your prayers were one of the reasons why I'm back again," he resumed. "The Lord said I still had more work to do, some of it with you all. But, please do me a favor," he started, tightening his smile and looking around the church with a slightly mischievous squint. "Unless you want to keep hearing me repeat the same things over and over and over again, please don't pray for me next time I die. Can you do me that small favor?" he asked, widening his smile and chuckling, prompting laughter and 'amens' around the church.

"Tell me, saints," he continued, reverting to his half smile. "And tell me the honest-to-God truth. You just said that you'd rather be in Heaven with Jesus right now than here sitting on those pews. Was that the truth?" The 'amens' were louder and even more plentiful than before.

Then, again cracking a wide smile, he said: "Then I'm sure you understand why I say please don't pray for me next time I die, right?" The congregation erupted in thunderous applause, laughter, and their loudest 'amens.'

His Permanent Trip to Heaven

After a few more months of witnessing for God, Mr. Melvin's health failed again and he was pronounced dead a third time. This time, however, his relatives and church brethren remembered his request and honored it. They didn't pray for him to return, at least not in the hospital; and he didn't.

We all knew that prayer had played a role in Mr. Melvin's two return trips from Heaven, because God told Mr. Melvin that in Heaven. But Mr. Melvin understood that it was only part of the reason why he came back. The other reason, and perhaps the most important, was that Mr. Melvin, like most other people who return to earth, still had unfinished work to complete.

CHAPTER III

A Teenager's Trip to Heaven

M s. Gina was a 15-year-old Caucasian-American girl who had led a mostly normal life as a teenager until her trip to Heaven. She was a good student in school, was active in several extracurricular activities, and had already made plans to attend college. She had many friends and was generally well liked. She had been raised with Christian values and teachings, and attended catholic mass every week with her family.

She Was Seriously Ill with Pneumonia

She was suffering from a severe bout of pneumonia that day and was rushed to the hospital. She was weak and feverish and soon lost consciousness:

"I woke up in the hospital and I knew right away that something was really wrong with me, because I couldn't move or open my eyes. But I could still hear and feel, so I knew the doctors were working hard trying to help me."

The Doctors Were Wrong When They Said She Was Gone

"I felt myself coming straight up out of my body and just floated there above it. And I could now see and hear everything, and I heard the doctors say they had lost me. But I knew they were wrong, because I was there right above them, and I felt fine. They just didn't understand that I was still alive."

She Flew Through a Dark "Hole" with a Bright Light at the End

"I watched them work on my body a little while longer. Then I felt myself flying through this dark space that looked like a long hole or something. When I got to the end, there was a real bright light right in front of me."

She Witnessed God and His Love

"I felt like this bright light was shining right through me. The light seemed like it was filled with love, and it was sending this love to me through the rays. It made me feel like it loved me no matter what I had done. I never knew that someone could feel that much peace and happiness. Somehow I knew that light was God and that He loved me no matter how much wrong I had done."

A Heavenly Landscape and Heavenly Sounds

"Then I noticed the landscape. It was kind of like a painting of a beautiful nature scene. It's hard to put it in words, but the colors and sounds were bright and alive.

She Wanted to Stay in Heaven with God

"I wanted to stay there with God very much, but the Light told me I had to go back to my life on earth because I still had a lot to do there before my life was over for good. But He told me this in a very loving and understanding way. And he wasn't communicating in normal words. It was more like thoughts. And I understood Him instantly.

He asked me if I understood why I had to go back, and I said yes, even though I really wanted to stay. Then, the next thing I knew, I was back in my body in the hospital room. I woke right up, and I was okay. "

Her Life is Different

The difference in Ms. Gina's life is very noticeable. She recovered completely from her illness. She is no longer afraid of dying, because she knows what awaits her in Heaven. She constantly seeks to strengthen her relationship with God, and prays very often. She is also more conscientious of how she treats other people, and does volunteer work to help others.

CHAPTER IV

At the Gates of Hell

Mr. Taf was an African-American in his early thirties at the time of his encounter with Hell. Although his early life had been greatly influenced by a strong Christian family, he was not a practicing Christian and was frequently involved in drug dealing. He continuously ignored the pleas of his family and friends to stop.

His hellish encounter happened one day after Mr. Taf had gotten into an argument with a group of his acquaintances over the whereabouts of some drug money:

They Attacked Him Viciously

"They were drug dealers I was involved with for about two years," he said. "They thought I had cheated them out of some money. I tried to explain that I didn't do it, but they wouldn't listen. They had their minds already made up and they came after me with knives and sticks.

"I ran down the street, but they caught me. I remember they jumped on me right beside a big dumpster. They just kept hitting and stabbing me. I was on the ground kicking and rolling and moving around trying to keep them from stabbing me in vital areas. I was catching a lot of the stabbing and hitting in my legs and arms, but not all of it.

"I was moving around as much as I could, hoping I could buy enough time for somebody to see what was happening and do something to help me or call the cops or something. I was screaming as loud as I could. But nobody came. It was like the street was deserted except for us, and it was dark outside."

He Resigned Himself to Death

"Then I started getting tired and weak real fast. I knew I was in danger of being killed. I was really scared, man. I was thinking to myself, 'I don't want to die.' But after a while, I just got too slow and weak to defend myself anymore. Then I collapsed on my stomach and couldn't move anymore. I knew I was dying.

He Left His Body Beside the Dumpster

"And then I felt like my spirit was rising up out of my body, and I didn't feel any more pain. As I rose higher and higher, it became harder and harder to see what was happening below. But I could see that the gang had stopped attacking my body and was running away from it. It was still there beside the dumpster. They must have thought it was dead, because it wasn't moving. But it was like that body that they had just killed wasn't me anymore. It almost seemed like somebody else."

He Felt Bad About the Life He Had Led

"I started feeling like I had let everybody down who cared about me. My family, my friends, and even myself. Then I thought about the fact that I was still young, and that made me feel even worse.

He Flew Through a Tunnel with No Light at the End

"Then I went through a long dark place that looked like a tunnel. And when I came out the other end, I was in the middle of nothing but spooky darkness. I mean, it felt scary. And I was wondering where I was and why I was there. Then I saw two big doors in front of me. I felt the urge to move toward them and I kind of floated in that direction."

He Saw Hellish Creatures

"Along the way, I saw some creatures that looked like little demons or something. They were dark gray things. They were very ugly creatures, like something you would see in a horror movie. And they scared me. I didn't know what they were going to do."

He Came to the Gates of Hell

"Then I reached the doors. I saw they were locked and I tried to push them open. The doors wouldn't budge, so I knocked as loud as I could, but nobody came. After I knocked a while longer, big slots came open in the middle of the doors. Through the slots I could see this bright hot fire burning, and I knew that it was Hell. I started thinking that I might have to go there, and that thought frightened me a lot. And I realized that if I went to Hell, it was because of the way I had lived on earth."

He Begged God for Another Chance

"I started crying to God to forgive me for all my sins. I promised Him that if he gave me another chance, I would change. If He would just give me my life back, I promised to turn my life around for Him.

Almost immediately after I prayed, I was back in my body in an ambulance with paramedics working on me. I could feel a lot of pain again, and my eyes were still shut. And I could hear the paramedics saying that I was breathing again, but I was in real bad shape and still might not make it."

A Miraculous Recovery

Mr. Taf's return to life was only his first miracle. The doctors had told him and his family that he would remain paralyzed for the rest of his life due to the placement of some of the stab wounds. They said he might regain a tiny amount of mobility in some parts of his limbs, but not nearly enough to walk.

But as he lay there in the hospital recovering, he constantly thought how grateful he was that God had given him another chance, and he followed through on his promise to God by accepting Jesus Christ as his personal savior.

Then after a while longer in the hospital, contrary to the grim prognosis of the doctors and the pessimism of his loved ones, Mr. Taf gradually recovered full control of his entire body. He became a living testimony to a higher healing power. He also became an active member of the church that he had grown up in.

CHAPTER V

The Light of Pure Love

Ms. Nita was a Puerto Rican Christian in her mid-sixties who frequently attended church. She was a widow and a loving mother of three children.

She Was Dying from a Cardiac Arrest

"I had a heart attack that day and the ambulance rushed me to the hospital. I had lost consciousness and I woke up on the operating table while the doctors were working on me. But I couldn't see anything or move my body."

She Left Her Body

"Then suddenly my spirit rose up out of my body. I felt really strange, but somehow I knew what was happening. I knew I was dying and that my spirit was coming out of my body. I floated over my body, and I could see the doctors working on it. And I heard one of them say that I was dead while my body was there on the operating table."

She Flew Through a "Long Dark Place" to a Bright Light that was Jesus

"Then in the next moment, I was in a long dark place and I flew through it until I came out at the end. When I came out, I was in the presence of a very bright light. As the light touched me I knew immediately who it was. It was Jesus. And He was bathing me in His love and His peace. The feelings of love and peace were very intense but still soft. The scenery all around me was colorful and very beautiful and there was sweet music kind of in the background."

She Wanted to Stay with Jesus but Had to Return to Earth

"I wanted stay there with Him forever, but He told me I had to go back. I kept begging Him, but He said I hadn't finished my work back on earth. Then I remember going back into my body still feeling sad and disappointed that I couldn't stay with the Lord."

Her Experience Changed Her Life

Besides her full recovery from her cardiac arrest, the most apparent effect of Ms. Gina's trip to Heaven was the dramatic increase in her enthusiasm in her work for God. She eagerly testifies about what she experienced in Heaven and what she knows about the reality of Jesus Christ.

She is more loving towards others and offers her help whenever and wherever she can. Her fear of dying is completely gone. She is also more aware of the short time she still has on earth to do God's work. So she tries to pack as much good into her remaining time as she can, all the while looking forward to the day when she returns to Heaven to live with God permanently.

CHAPTER VI

She Wanted to Go with Jesus

M s. Lizzie was a devout African-American Christian in her late fifties at the time of her trip to Heaven. She had suffered from various physical ailments over the previous few years, including occasional epileptic seizures. She was very active in her church and was known for being very enthusiastic in church-related activities. She was always ready to help in any way that she could. She was also a devoted mother of six children, whom she raised for the most part without much help from her wayward and mostly absent husband.

A Convergence of Physical and Emotional Problems Led to Her Death

"This happened on a day when I had a lot on my mind. I had a seizure, a stroke, and a heart attack all at the same time. I think this was brought on by all the stress in my life at the time. I felt so much stress. When it first happened, I was unconscious. But later I was conscious in the hospital, but I couldn't move or anything. I could hear what people were saying, and I heard the doctor tell my family that I was in a coma and probably would not survive. And he said that even if I did survive, I wouldn't be able to do anything on my own. He said that because of brain damage I wouldn't be anything more than a vegetable."

She Went to Heaven and Saw Biblical Figures

"Then somehow I found myself on the other side, in the spirit world. One of the first things I saw when I got there were the "four and twenty elders" spoken of in the New Testament in the book of Revelations. I knew they were the four and twenty elders by the way I felt and because I recognized them by the way they looked. I could see parts of their faces just like I'm looking at you now" (she was telling me her story).

The following verse is what Ms. Lizzie was referring to by the "four and twenty elders":

> **Revelation 4:4** (NIV)
>
> *"Surrounding the throne were twenty-four other thrones, and seated on them were twenty-four elders. They were dressed in white and had crowns of gold on their heads."*

Considering how the Scriptures say they were dressed and the fact that they wore crowns and sat on thrones in Heaven, these elders may be representatives of the Church who were with Christ in Heaven. This would explain why Ms. Lizzie saw them during her trip to Heaven.

Then she described the environment around her in Heaven:

A Peaceful Environment with Jesus

"Everything there was so peaceful, and there were bright lights all over. Then I heard Jesus say that I was dead. I knew without a doubt that it was Jesus and I wanted to go with Him. Right then I was between Heaven and Earth, but I wanted to go with Jesus."

She Had More Work to Do on Earth

"But then He told me that I couldn't go with Him because I have more work to do on Earth. The work He was talking about was gaining more souls for Him. This meant working with people who were down and pulling them out of the fire. They are people like drug addicts and prostitutes and such."

She Did Not Want to Return to Earth

"But I really didn't want to come back because everything was so peaceful there. Then when Jesus got ready to send me back, I saw myself floating above my body. I saw the body there. And when I got back, when my spirit got back into the body, I could feel the body's weight all of a sudden."

"The doctors had said that even if I survived, I wouldn't be anything more than a vegetable because of brain damage. And, as you see, the doctors were very wrong. I'm alive and I'm not a vegetable. God healed me!"

She was right. Even the doctors considered it a miracle. She not only survived, she did so without the slightest hint of any remaining brain damage. She was completely healed!

It Made Her More Aware of The Need to Treat Others Well

"Besides healing me, God changed my life in other ways through this experience. Now, I check my life more than I ever did before to make sure everything is alright between me and other people. For example, if I know I did something to offend you, I've got to come to you and make it right, no matter what it is or how bad it hurts. I have to make those wrongs right. It makes me more conscious of what I'm doing. I'm just more alert.

And I'm on a mission to complete what God wants me to do. And I think I had that experience because God wanted to make me more sure of how real eternal life is. And it really is. I think the least little thing can keep me from the Kingdom, the least little thing. He let me realize this more and more, and that's no joke."

It Made Her Aware of How Important All People Are to God

"This experience also made me love people more, and made me realize how important everybody is. Man is so precious in the sight of God, and I mean everybody. Even drug addicts, prostitutes, and other people who people think are no good. You'd be surprised how important every person really is. Everybody is very important to God."

CHAPTER VII

An Agnostic Found God in the Mediterranean

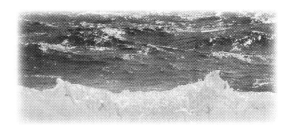

M r. El-Amin was a young Egyptian graduate student in his early twenties at the time of his otherworldly trip. He was considered a kind and considerate person by his friends, and he was very intellectual and philosophical about many things in life, including spirituality. He was respectful of other people's philosophies and religions, but he openly told his friends that he did not believe in God. Instead, he described himself as somewhere "between an atheist and a borderline agnostic."

He Was Swimming in the Mediterranean When It Happened

"I had been swimming for quite a while, and the sun had set before I realized it. You see, I had lost track of time. But I knew it was getting very late, so I started swimming back. I wasn't that far from the shore, but then the weather started getting bad and the waves were very strong. Also a strong current was flowing outward to sea, so I was actually being pulled farther out than I was before.

"Then I began to feel very desperate, because, no matter how hard I tried, I was not making any progress forward. And on top of that, I was getting very tired. I then screamed loudly for help, but no one came. I felt like I was the only person in the world right then. I was so alone. I looked all around and strained my eyes to see where the people were, but I saw no one at all. I think everyone else had gone for cover, because it had started raining and the waves were strong."

He Knew He was About to Die

"Finally, after struggling for such a long time and being exhausted and frustrated and terrified, I just gave up. I no longer resisted the current. I decided to just let it take me wherever it flowed, because all my efforts would be futile anyway. I just resigned myself to drowning. I knew I had seen my last day on earth. Then I think I must have lost consciousness."

He Stood Before God and Reviewed His Life

"Then I was awake and I felt like I was floating up out of my body and above the waves. I also saw some people in boats moving in my direction, apparently to rescue me. But that didn't seem to matter much anymore, because now I realized that my body was not really me.

And then I saw a very strange bright light. It didn't blind me, but it was very bright and full of love and peace. I knew immediately that it was God, even though I previously did not believe in God.

"Then He directed my attention to something in front of me and I saw my life begin to appear before my eyes. I saw scenes from different times in my life. It was like watching a movie. What I saw made me feel sad and remorseful, because I knew that I had been so wrong about life and God."

He Returned to His Body on the Shore

"After my feelings of remorse, I felt myself being pulled back on the shore in my body, where the lifeguards had brought me. When I opened my eyes, I could see a crowd of people around me. Most of them were smiling, and they told me how relieved they were because I wasn't breathing for several minutes."

He Made a Drastic Change

Mr. El-Amin underwent a number of drastic attitudinal and spiritual changes as a result of his experience: He is now a firm believer in God and witnesses for God to his friends, relatives, and others. He no longer fears death and knows that the most important part of his existence comes after physical death.

In addition, he now knows that life on earth is not a topic for philosophical speculation but rather a place where God put us to allow us to control our spiritual destinies by how we live our earthly lives. He also enthusiastically tells others how he found God in the Mediterranean.

CHAPTER VIII

Angels Sang to Her

M s. Virginia was a devout African-American Christian in her sixties when she took her first trip to Heaven. Separated from her husband, she was a devoted mother of eight children whom she raised mostly alone. She had been chronically ill for the past several years, suffering from asthma and various other debilitating ailments. But she didn't let her physical problems dampen her spirit or her ministry in church. She preached occasionally, but her main ministry for God was in her music. She sang and played the piano with so much energy and enthusiasm that people who didn't know her personally could never guess that she was suffering physically.

But on one fateful day at home, while Ms. Virginia was already battling a severe case of pneumonia, an acute asthma attack struck. The combination of the two left her barely breathing and very close to death. The paramedics arrived quickly, placed her in the ambulance and worked feverishly to keep her alive on the way to the hospital.

She Knew She Was Dying

"I had asthma and pneumonia together and I was in intensive care. I felt my breath leaving me and I knew I was dying." "That feeling I had was something you just can't express. I could hear the sound of people's feet running around, and I heard them saying they were losing me. And when that feeling hit me, I knew I was on my way out and I couldn't breathe. The doctors said I had stopped breathing for several minutes."

She Left Her Body and Went Through a "Dark Place"

"Then I could feel myself leaving my body. That was a feeling I just can't describe. I just came out of my whole body. And then I went through this kind of dark place. And then it seemed like I was up in a place like outer space standing before God."

She Wanted to Return to Earth

"When I was up there, I was asking God to forgive me the whole time. And I know this happened to me because I wasn't doing enough for God. And it seemed that I could hear my own voice asking God for forgiveness. And after I asked for a while, he snapped me back to earth in my body just as quick as you could pop your finger. And when I got back here to earth, this place looked like a brand new world to me. Everything looked new."

God Communicated Without Words

"And even after I returned to my body, God kept bringing it to my attention that I hadn't done enough for Him. That was why I had this experience. He let me know why. It was like He told me, but it wasn't in words. He kept bringing to mind that I should have done what He wanted me to do." So I learned something, and I tell everyone that I get a chance to tell that if God tells you to do something, you'd better do it."

Angels Sang to Her in the Hospital

"Just after I got back, the strangest thing happened to me while I was still in the hospital. Every night when I was alone in bed there, I would hear beautiful music and singing. Something told me they were angels. Angels were singing above my bed! I think maybe God was giving me some comfort after what I went through. And I was just so happy the whole time!"

The Experience Changed Her Life

"This experience changed my life a great deal. First of all, I was no longer afraid to die. Then I started doing the things that I should have been doing all along. I started witnessing more for Him and preaching His word more."

A Different Type of Heavenly Experience?

Ms. Virginia was with God, so we have to assume that she was in some part of Heaven. But she experienced some of the environmental beauty of Heaven in a slightly different manner than others. That is, she heard Heavenly music *after* she left Heaven rather than during her trip there. Another somewhat unusual part of her experience was the fact that, unlike others, she didn't beg to *stay* in Heaven. On the contrary, she wanted to leave so she could return to earth.

Why was her experience different? Well, comparing Ms. Virginia's experience to that of others, I'd say that a major reason for the difference here is related to her own knowledge that she had unfinished work to complete on earth. That is, other travelers to Heaven had begged to stay there and had to be told by God that they had to complete unfinished work.

Ms. Virginia, on the other hand, already knew she had work to finish on earth before she was told by God. And she didn't only ask to return to earth; she also asked for forgiveness for not doing everything she should have done on earth, and asked for the opportunity to return to her body to finish it. This preoccupation with leaving Heaven may have distracted her from marveling at any Heavenly scenery that may have been around her.

CHAPTER IX

Rescued from the Lake of Fire

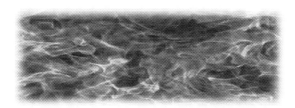

M r. Melvin's case was the most amazing case I had ever heard of in terms of the number of times he died and went to Heaven. But Mr. Robert's case was the most amazing in another way—the sheer amount of mangling his physical body had to recover from.

Mr. Robert, an African-American, was similar to Mr. Taf in the destructiveness of his lifestyle at the time of his experience. He was in his mid-twenties and had been raised with Christian teachings, but never really practiced them. He had gone to church on most Sundays, but only because he was pressured to go.

At times, he showed little regard for his own safety and even less for the safety of others. For example, he would drive recklessly at high speeds while intoxicated. It was one of those wild rides that led to his hellish experience:

He had just left a Friday-evening party with two of his friends. Everyone had been drinking, and as he often did, Mr. Robert had drunk so much that he staggered while walking.

He Wouldn't Slow Down

"My friends knew how heavy my foot got when I was drinking, so they kept telling me to let somebody else drive. But being stubborn like I was, I didn't listen to them. They knew they couldn't change my mind, so they started telling me not to drive too fast. I agreed and for a while I drove at a safe speed.

"But after I drove for a while, I got into this wild mood and I wanted to drive real fast. They were yelling real loud for me to slow down, but hearing them yell only excited me more and made me want to go even faster. I think I had the gas pedal either on the floor or pretty close to it. Thinking back, I think I must have been crazy to drive that fast because it was real dark and hard to see on the road."

Then He Lost Control

"One of the last things I remember was that I didn't turn into a curve soon enough and I tried to make up for it by turning the wheel too hard and too far. I vaguely remember the car sliding off the road and my friends screaming. But I don't remember anything after that. My friends told me that the accident happened right afterwards. They said the car slid off the left shoulder down a hill and rolled about four or five times."

He Was a Bloody Mangled Mess and Lost Part of His Brain

"I was thrown out of the driver's side window. The paramedics said I must have been thrown out like a slingshot, because the medical report said I landed about twenty feet from where the car had stopped.

"My friends and the doctors I talked to said I was a bloody mess with all kinds of cuts and bruises and broken bones all over my body.

They said it was a wonder I didn't die instantly, especially because of the injuries to my skull and brain. They said after I flew through the air, my head slammed into the tree that they found me under. My skull was split open and had a big hole in it on the left side in the back. And they said pieces of my brain came out of the hole.

"The paramedics said when they first looked at me, my body was in such bad shape, especially my head, they were thinking of not trying to revive me at first, because they thought it would just be a waste of time. But they decided to try for a while and they said they got a weak pulse from me. Then they rushed me to the hospital."

He Lost More of His Brain and His Life on the Operating Table

"And then the doctors had to remove some more of my brain on the operating table because part of it was mangled and still had stuff in it like dirt and bark from the tree trunk. They said while I was on the operating table I stopped breathing and my heart stopped beating. They said I was dead."

Mr. Robert Was Outside His Body the Whole Time

"But that wasn't really me in the hospital. I wasn't in my body after the accident. I don't remember hitting the tree, but sometime after it happened I felt my spirit rush out of my body and float up above it. I knew it was my fault that the whole thing happened. I saw that my friends were hurt, too, but not as bad as I was.

Mr. Robert's Doctors and Family Gave up on Him

"After a while the doctors got my heart beating again and put me on a respirator, but they said I was in a coma and my vital signs were still very weak. I saw them working on me a lot, and I heard them say there was no hope because they couldn't repair all the brain damage or replace all the brain tissue I lost.

They said I was already a vegetable and would stay that way even if I somehow was able to survive. Then they told my family they were giving up on me because there was no hope, so they should take me off the respirator and start making funeral arrangements. My family believed the doctors and they told them to unhook my body from the respirator.

He Flew Through a Tunnel, and Encountered Hellish Beings

"After they unhooked my body from the respirator, it stopped breathing and they said I was gone. Then I suddenly felt myself being pulled away through something that looked like a dark tunnel, and I was heading for an opening at the far end.

When I came out the other end, these little creatures were there. It seemed like they were there just to meet me. They were scary, ugly little things. I knew they were demons and I wanted to get away from them. I started backing away, but I lost my footing and fell near the edge of something that looked like a cliff. I had to grab the edge of it to keep from falling off."

He Nearly Fell into Hellish Fire

"While I was hanging off the cliff, I looked down and saw what looked like a giant sea of hot fire. And the flames seemed to be reaching up toward me. And they were getting closer and closer. I was really afraid and I was desperately trying to pull myself up from the edge. But then the demons started stepping on my hands, trying to make me lose my grip."

He Was Saved from Hell by Jesus

"Just as I was about to give up and fall down into the fire, this spirit made of pure bright light appeared above me. And the spirit of light reached down and lifted me up from the edge of the cliff. Then the demons just disappeared. The spirit stayed there for a while in front of me, just looking at me, and I could feel this strong love shining out from the light. I immediately knew it was Jesus Christ. I was taught about Him in church, but, I never really believed He was real till then. Somehow I just knew it was Jesus Christ."

Jesus Made Him Review His Life

"Right after I thought about who He was, He started showing me things that I did in my life starting from when I was much younger. It was like watching a movie of myself. I saw things I had done that I had forgotten about till then. I felt very sad and ashamed of so many things in my life. I realized how irresponsible I had been and I was just so sorry and humble.

Then Jesus told me, without words, that I would soon be returning to my body. He made me understand that if I didn't change my life, He wouldn't rescue me from the lake of fire next time. I promised Him that I would change."

A Miracle that Defied all Logic and Medicine

Mr. Robert did indeed return to life on earth, and he was not a human vegetable, to the amazement of everyone, especially the doctors who had worked on him. He started breathing again without the respirator, and his other vital signs rapidly recovered. After a period of rehabilitation, he completely recovered all of his mental and physical functions and abilities. Eventually, aside from the metal plate in his skull, there was no sign that he had been such a physical mess.

The doctors were astounded beyond words or belief. His entire body had been broken and mangled, a great portion of his brain was missing, and a great deal of his remaining brain was damaged. So how could he have survived, much less regained his normal mind and physical functions? He was a walking miracle in every sense of the word.

A Drastic Change in His Life

True to his promise to God, Mr. Robert changed his ways. And I mean drastically. He became a very considerate, respectful, and compassionate person, especially to women. In addition, he became a practicing Christian who frequently witnessed for God by presenting himself and his experience as a living testimony to the power of God and the reality of Heaven and Hell.

PART III

Other Questions about Heaven and Hell

CHAPTER X

Who Goes to Heaven and Who Goes to Hell?

N ow that we've confirmed the existence of Heaven and Hell, the next question is who goes to which place? Yes, the Bible tells us that those who follow Christ will go to Heaven, but how do we know who's really following Christ? How does a real follower of Christ behave?

Can They All Be Real Followers of Christ?

Can all people who call themselves Christians be real followers of Christ? I guess we could say that it's theoretically possible, but is it possible in practical human terms? For example, if 10 people claim to be Christians, yet differ vastly in important ways like their morality and how they treat other people, can all 10 be real followers of Christ?

These are questions that seem quite difficult when we pose them. But, believe it or not, they're actually quite easy to answer—with the right checklist, of course.

A Checklist of Real Christian Qualities?

Yes indeed. We have a checklist to identify real followers of Christ. And we can use it on ourselves or anyone else. The Bible tells us that all real followers of Christ must show the following three qualities: 1) they must have salvation and ongoing faith in God, 2) they must do good works with the right attitude, and 3) above all, they must obey the two greatest commandments.

Just to make sure we all understand the qualities in this checklist in the same way, let's clarify them briefly:

I. Salvation and Ongoing Faith in God

The most basic and clearest of the three qualities of a true follower of Christ are salvation and faith. Salvation is the grace and eternal life that we receive as a result of Christ's sacrifice for our sins after we repent and accept Jesus Christ as our personal savior. Faith is belief in Christ, which enables us to receive God's grace and salvation. These verses make this point even clearer:

> **John 3:16** (NIV): *For God so loved the world that he gave his one and only Son, that whoever believes in him shall not perish but have eternal life.*

> **Ephesians 2:8** *(NIV): For it is by grace you have been saved, through faith—and this is not from yourselves, it is the gift of God*

> **Romans 10:4** (NIV): *Christ is the culmination of the law so that there may be righteousness for everyone who believes.*

II. Good Works with the Right Attitude

The second quality of a true Christian is doing good deeds with the right attitude. Christ Himself did a lot of good works in the form of teaching, preaching, and working miracles; and He asks us to do whatever good works we can as well:

> **Matthew 5:16** (NIV): *In the same way, let your light shine before others, that they may see your good deeds and glorify your Father in heaven.*

> **Matthew 25:34-36** (NIV): *Then the King will say to those on his right, 'Come, you who are blessed by my Father; take your inheritance, the kingdom prepared for you since the creation of the world.*

> *For I was hungry and you gave me something to eat, I was thirsty and you gave me something to drink, I was a stranger and you invited me in,*

> *I needed clothes and you clothed me, I was sick and you looked after me, I was in prison and you came to visit me.*

Are Good Works With a Bad Attitude Still Meaningful?

Excellent question. What if we do what other people consider 'good works,' but our hearts and minds are in the wrong places when we do those works? In other words, what if we did good deeds, for example, just to show off and impress people? Well, according to the only document with the divine authority to answer that question—the Bible—we would just be wasting our time and efforts:

Matthew 6:1-3 (NIV): *Be careful not to practice your righteousness in front of others to be seen by them. If you do, you will have no reward from your Father in heaven.*

So when you give to the needy, do not announce it with trumpets, as the hypocrites do in the synagogues and on the streets, to be honored by others. Truly I tell you, they have received their reward in full.

But when you give to the needy, do not let your left hand know what your right hand is doing, So that your giving may be in secret. Then your Father, who sees what is done in secret, will reward you.

The Right Attitude for Christians—Love and Cheerfulness?

Yes indeed. The attitude that real followers of Christ should have when doing good works is one that shows love and cheerfulness:

1 John 3:18 (NIV): *Dear children, let us not love with words or speech but with actions and in truth.*

I Corinthians 13:3 (NKJV): *And though I bestow all my goods to feed the poor, and though I give my body to be burned, but have not love, it profits me nothing.*

And love gives us the right frame of mind for giving:

2 Corinthians 9:7 (NIV): *Each of you should give what you have decided in your heart to give, not* *reluctantly or under compulsion, for God loves a cheerful giver.*

III. Obeying the Two Greatest Commandments

Of the three qualities of a true Christian, the most important is obeying the two greatest commandments. Jesus Himself said these two commandments form the basis of all of the Ten Commandments and all other religious laws in the Old and New Testaments:

> **Matthew 22:37-40** (NIV)
>
> *Jesus replied: "'Love the Lord your God with all your heart and with all your soul and with all your mind.'*
>
> *This is the first and greatest commandment.*
>
> *And the second is like it: 'Love your neighbor as yourself.'*
>
> *All the Law and the Prophets hang on these two commandments."*

Clearly, Christ tells us in these verses that in order to live a real Christian life we must love God above all else and love our neighbors as we love ourselves.

The Commandments of Love?

Yes, these are the two commandments of love. The previous section stressed the need for love in our attitude when doing good works. These two commandments go a step further and tell us to have love in all situations relating to God and to other people.

But What Kind of Love?

The Merriam-Webster dictionary defines love as a "feeling of strong or constant affection" for someone.

In English, we use the same word 'love' to describe several different types of strong affection.

In Greek, however, there are several words for different types of love. We can see three of those in the New Testament. For example:

- **στοργή** (storge) This is familial love such as what parents and children feel for each other. In Romans 1:31 a negative form of this word (ἀστόργους—astorgous) is used, and literally means 'no love.'
- **φιλία** (philia): This is the type of love generally called brotherly love, and is used for affection between siblings and close friends. A form of it can be seen in Romans 12:10 in the phrase τῇ φιλαδελφίᾳ (te philadelphia), which literally means 'in brotherly love.'
- **ἀγάπη** (agape): This is considered the highest form of love. It is the spiritual love expressed by God for us, by us for God, and by us for one another.

In nearly all New Testament references to a*gape,* the spiritual sense of love is meant. And, of course, the love referred to in the two greatest commandments is *agape.*

Love is also a Divine Quality?

Indeed it is. In addition to being the affectionate energy that God shares with us, love is also part of God Himself that God shares with us.

What do we mean? We mean that the love that is shared between God and man is a quality of God. It is part of His nature, His being. As a matter of fact, the Bible tells us that God *is* love:

1 John 4:7, 8 (NIV)

Dear friends, let us love one another, for love comes from God. Everyone who loves has been born of God and knows God. Whoever does not love does not know God, because God is love.

Sharing Love is a Divine Activity?

Absolutely. If God is love, and we express love to God and to other people, doesn't that mean that we are essentially sharing an important aspect of God's energy and nature with them? Thus, by showing love, we are, in a very real sense, carrying out a divine activity.

So when we think of loving God and other people, we should do so with the awareness that love is not just an idea or an emotion, but also divine energy.

The Two Greatest Commandments Lead to a True Christian Life?

Absolutely. If we really internalize these two commandments, we cannot help but follow the Ten Commandments and all of His New Testament teachings, including all of His doctrine of living a Christian life. This means that following Christ would come automatically if we apply these two commandments in our lives.

In other words, by obeying these two commandments, we automatically have the right attitudes and behaviors towards God and towards other people, regardless of what types of interactions we happen to be engaged in with them.

Loving God

This means that, if we really love God above all else, then we will behave at all times in a manner that God would approve of. This includes automatically obeying the first commandment, which says we should have no other Gods before Jehovah; the second commandment, which says we should not worship anything other than God; the third, which says that we should not misuse His name; and the fourth, which says we should remember that the Sabbath is the special day that we set aside for God.

Loving Others

By the same token, if we really love our neighbors as ourselves, then we would automatically refrain from doing anything to hurt them.

For instance, we would obey the sixth commandment by not murdering anyone; the seventh by not committing adultery with our neighbor's spouse, the eighth by not stealing from our neighbors, the ninth by not lying on our neighbors, and the tenth by not coveting our neighbors' possessions. This means that if we love others as we love ourselves, we would be happy that they possess what they have, not envious, right?

We would also love our neighbors regardless of their skin color, gender, age, or any other genetic qualities. And we would gladly help any of them in their time of need and would not feel the urge to show the public that we are helping them. This is because our help would come from our hearts, not the desire for an earthly reward.

Follow the Commandments of Love

If we allow these two commandments of love to steer our hearts, minds, and behavior, we will not only automatically be true followers of our Lord and Savior Jesus Christ, but we will also reap our ultimate reward—being with God in Heaven.

CHAPTER XI

Once Saved Always Saved?

An Unresolvable Debate?

Most of us have undoubtedly heard both sides of this still-unsettled debate: One side says that once we accept Christ as our personal savior, we will remain saved and Heaven-bound, regardless of what we do. The other side is convinced that if we knowingly sin and don't repent, we lose our salvation and will not make it to Heaven. So who is right? Which side of this seemingly non-ending controversy should we take? Let's review the Biblical evidence that each side uses to justify its claim and then compare notes:

Bible Verses that Support "Once Saved Always Saved"?

Those who believe that "once saved always saved" will often quote certain Bible verses to prove their point. The verses they use the most include the following:

John 3:16 (NIV)

For God so loved the world that he gave his one and only Son, that whoever believes in him shall not perish but have eternal life.

Titus 3:5 (NIV)

He saved us, not because of righteous things we had done, but because of his mercy. He saved us through the washing of rebirth and renewal by the Holy Spirit.

Ephesians 2:8, 9 (NIV)

For it is by grace you have been saved, through faith—and this is not from yourselves, it is the gift of God—not by works, so that no one can boast.

John 10:28, 29 (NIV)

I give them eternal life, and they shall never perish; no one will snatch them out of my hand.

John 8:38, 39 (NIV)

For I am convinced that neither death nor life, neither angels nor demons, neither the present nor the future, nor any powers, neither height nor depth, nor anything else in all creation, will be able to separate us from the love of God that is in Christ Jesus our Lord.

Do Those Verses Really Support "Once Saved Always Saved"?

I'm sure we can all agree that the Bible verses we've just read support a number of familiar Gospel teachings. For example, they support the teaching that salvation and eternal life come not from our works, but from our belief and faith in Jesus as the only way to salvation, and from God's love and grace through the sacrifice of His Son Jesus Christ. They also support the teaching that nothing can separate the sheep, which are us, from the love of the shepherd, which is God in Christ Jesus.

But do these verses really support "once saved always saved"? As far as my own answer is concerned, I'll say the following for now--be careful and don't take risks. And I'll tell you why I said that a little later in this section.

Why Others Say "Once Saved Always Saved" Is Not True

Those who say that the verses we just read do not support "once saved always saved" say that their position is supported by at least two things: 1) the grammar used in the Greek word for "believe" in John 3:16 indicates conditional salvation and 2) Many Bible verses show that salvation is conditional and not permanent. Are they right? The only way to know is by reviewing their evidence. First, let's look at the Greek word for 'believe':

The Grammar of the Word "Believe" in John 3:16: The Greek verb form πιστευων (pisteuon) comes from the verb πιστευω (pisteuo), which means to have belief, trust, or faith in something. Grammatically, πιστευων is the present active participle (in English, this is a verb with an '-ing' ending, as in 'reading' or 'writing') of πιστευω. So πιστευων literally means 'believing.'

In these verses, πιστευων appears in the phrase πας ο πιστευων (pas ho pisteuon), which literally means 'each (or every) person believing,' in other words, 'each person who is believing' in the sense of a timeless and continuous present tense. In other words, right now, at this very moment that we happen to be in, and in each moment continuously until we die.

So, by referring to our belief in the timeless present, these verses connote that some of us who believed at a certain time in the past may not be believing right now or in some present moment as life goes on.

Therefore, those who dispute "once saved always saved" believe that verses like John 3:16, John 3:36 and others apply only to people who still believe, not to those who may have believed in the past, but no longer do. In other words, they say this verb form supports the idea of conditional salvation.

Bible Verses that Disprove "Once Saved Always Saved"?

Opponents of "once saved always saved" also say that the following verses are among many that prove that salvation is conditional, not permanent:

James 5:19, 20 (NIV)

My brothers and sisters, if one of you should wander from the truth and someone should bring that person back, remember this: Whoever turns a sinner from the error of their way will save them from death and cover over a multitude of sins

Hebrews 10:26-27 (NIV)

If we deliberately keep on sinning after we have received the knowledge of the truth, no sacrifice for sins is left, but only a fearful expectation of judgment and of raging fire that will consume the enemies of God.

2 Peter 2:20-22 (NIV)

If they have escaped the corruption of the world by knowing our Lord and Savior Jesus Christ and are again entangled in it and are overcome, <u>they are worse off at the end than they were at the beginning</u>.

<u>It would have been better for them not to have known the way of righteousness</u>, than to have known it and then to turn their backs on the sacred command that was passed on to them.

1 Timothy 4:16 (NIV)

Watch your life and doctrine closely. <u>Persevere in them, because if you do, you will save both yourself and your hearers</u>.

Colossians 1:21-23 (NIV)

Once you were alienated from God and were enemies in your minds because of your evil behavior.

But now he has reconciled you by Christ's physical body through death to present you holy in his sight, without blemish and free from accusation — <u>if you continue in your faith</u>, established and firm, and do not move from the hope held out in the gospel.

Romans 11:19-22 (NIV)

Consider therefore the kindness and sternness of God: sternness to those who fell, but kindness to you, <u>provided that you continue in his kindness. Otherwise, you also will be cut off.</u>

And if they do not persist in unbelief, they will be grafted in, for <u>God is able to graft them in again.</u>

1 Corinthians 15:2 (NIV)

By this gospel you are saved, <u>if you hold firmly to the word I preached to you.</u> Otherwise, you have believed in vain.

The opponents of "once saved always saved" say that these last few verses warn us that Christians can indeed lose their salvation if they deliberately commit sins without repenting. They believe that these verses, therefore, prove that salvation is conditional and not permanent.

So Which Side is Right?

Remember this: This is the one and only issue in this book on which I will not declare a a clear and firm position. Why not? Well, because it happens to be the one and only issue in this book on which I can make my point without having to declare a clear and firm position. And here's why:

Earlier in this section, I advised us to be careful and to not take risks? Well, I said that because, regardless of where we stand on the "once saved always saved" debate and how sure we are of our positions on it, the bottom line for us as Christians is making sure we have salvation when we depart this life.

If "once saved always saved" is true, and we retain our salvation no matter what, then that's good for all of us who have accepted Christ as our personal savior. But what if it's not true? If it's not, a lot of us will be in big trouble after we pass on if we're not living a true Christian life. That's why my main point, again, is this:

Why take unnecessary chances? If we knowingly sin, what harm would it do to simply repent, ask Christ for forgiveness, and resolve to live a better Christian life? It might make an eternity of difference.

CHAPTER XII

Salvation for Those Who Don't or Can't Know Jesus?

One of the most frequently asked questions regarding who goes to Heaven or Hell is about those who have either not heard about Jesus or not heard enough to understand who He is or what His Gospel is. There are a number of reasons why many people today may know nothing at all about Jesus or His Gospel. For example, people in remote tribal areas, people in repressive societies that might prohibit the dissemination of information on certain religions, and people who believe so deeply in their own religions that they have no motivation or opportunity to learn of others. In such cases, where will God send those people when they pass? Will it be Heaven or Hell? Or maybe some place else?

Rather than simply speculate about what God might do, let's review some Bible verses related to this issue to help us draw more informed conclusions:

Does the Bible Excuse Those Who Don't Know Jesus?

Romans 10:14 (NIV)

How, then, can they call on the one they have not believed in? And how can they believe in the one of whom they have not heard? And how can they hear without someone preaching to them?

Romans 10:17 (NIV)

Consequently, faith comes from hearing the message, and the message is heard through the word about Christ.

Two Messages from Romans 10

- First, these verses clearly acknowledge the impossibility of repenting and believing in Jesus without first knowing about Jesus.
- Second, these verses clearly imply that those who have not heard about Jesus will not be held accountable for not believing in Him. The following verses confirm this implication:

2 Peter 2: 20, 21 (NIV)

If they have escaped the corruption of the world by knowing our Lord and Savior Jesus Christ and are again entangled in it and are overcome, they are worse off at the end than they were at the beginning.

It would have been better for them not to have known the way of righteousness, than to have known it and

then to turn their backs on the sacred command that
was passed on to them..

Implication Confirmed in 2 Peter

The underlined portions of these last two verses clearly confirm the second message in Romans 10 above that those who don't know Jesus are better off than those who know Him and turn their backs on Him.

Correct me if I'm wrong, but if those who don't know Jesus are "better off" in this situation, doesn't that imply that they have at least a chance to go to Heaven?

Does God Judge the Works of those Who Don't Know Jesus?

So, based on the verses we've just reviewed, wouldn't it be reasonable to assume that Romans 10 really does say that people cannot be judged on whether they follow Gospel teachings if they have never even heard the Gospel? And taking this assumption one step further, if they are not judged by whether they follow Gospel teachings, doesn't that leave only their works to judge them by?

Here are two verses that say just that:

Luke 12:47, 48 (NIV)

The servant who knows the master's will and does not get ready or does not do what the master wants will be beaten with many blows.

But the one who does not know and does things deserving punishment will be beaten with few blows.

Three Important Messages in Luke 12

- First, the verses clearly say that we are judged by both what we do and what we know.
- Second, verse 48 tells us that what we know is so important that people who sin and don't know Jesus will be better off than those who sin and do know Him.
- Third, and more to the point of this section, the two verses inform us that if we have never heard of Jesus, we are judged by the things that we know are right and wrong.

Romans 2: 14-16 (NIV)

Indeed, when Gentiles, who do not have the law, do by nature things required by the law, they are a law for themselves, even though they do not have the law.

They show that the requirements of the law are written on their hearts, their consciences also bearing witness, and their thoughts sometimes accusing them and at other times even defending them.

This will take place on the day when God judges people's secrets through Jesus Christ, as my gospel declares.

Three Important Messages in Romans 2

- First, these verses acknowledge the fact that many non-Jews, aka Gentiles, had no way of knowing God's written law; and the law was basically the written Old Testament teachings that Jews followed to ensure that they lived a good enough life to go to Heaven.

- Second, they tell us that it is possible for people to do and to be judged by many of the same good things that are required by the law, even if they don't have access to the actual written law.
- Third, they seem to tell us that that people who don't know the Gospel of Christ can indeed go to Heaven if their hearts and works are judged good enough by God.

What About People Who Cannot Know Jesus?

In the following section, we'll discuss two groups of people who absolutely cannot know Christ or His Gospel:

Babies and the Mentally Ill?

What about babies? They are certainly too young to know or to understand the Gospel. And what about adults who are too mentally ill to know or understand the Gospel? Will these two groups be sent to Hell for their total inability to know Jesus?:

> ### Deuteronomy 1:39 (NIV)
>
> *And the little ones that you said would be taken captive, your children who do not yet know good from bad....*

This verse describes young children as being unable to distinguish between good and evil. And I'm sure we can all recall some of the many verses in this chapter that say that those who don't know the Gospel or the difference between good and evil will not be held accountable for it.

Mark 10:14 (NIV)

When Jesus saw this, he was indignant. He said to them, "Let the little children come to me, and do not hinder them, for the kingdom of God belongs to such as these.

Here Jesus teaches us that young children, who do not yet know what evil is and are, therefore, completely innocent, are part of the Kingdom of God, meaning that if they died that young, they would go to Heaven.

Romans 5:13 (NIV)

To be sure, sin was in the world before the law was given, but sin is not charged against anyone's account where there is no law.

This verse applies to both young children and the very mentally ill, because neither has knowledge and understanding of the law, let alone of Jesus and His Gospel. And, as this verse stresses, no sin is counted against such people. And if that is the case, won't they go to Heaven?

Is It Really So Urgent to Spread the Word to Them?

So, if people who don't know the Gospel could still make it to Heaven if their works are good enough, would it really be that urgent to disseminate the Gospel to them? Good question, and here's my answer:

Absolutely, yes! Hearing or reading the Gospel would do three extremely important things for those who do not yet know Christ:

First and foremost, it would open the door to their salvation, which would remove the need to worry about whether their works alone were good enough to make it into Heaven.

Second, it would provide them with instructions on how to live a good Christian life after receiving salvation and how to strengthen their spirituality, and would ensure that they did not lose their salvation.

Third, it would enable them to participate in spreading the Gospel to still others who have not yet heard of it, in order to give even more people the opportunity to go to Heaven.

Final Thoughts on This Issue

In summary, not only does it make rational sense that people everywhere can go to Heaven even if they have not been fortunate enough to have heard about Jesus, but it also makes spiritual sense, and we have seen a number of Bible verses that confirm it.

Does that mean that anyone who has never heard of Jesus automatically goes to Heaven? No, not at all. Even though they may not be held accountable for following the written Gospel per se, the Bible (e.g. Romans 2) tells us that they will be held accountable for following high standards that they do know, including their own consciences.

This means they still have to meet high standards of good works and spirituality, and have to continue doing so for the duration of their lives to even have a chance to go to Heaven. In essence, they have to meet the same strict standards, relatively speaking, that the Bible sets for those who already know Christ.

Another Controversial Question About Who Can Go to Heaven?

After establishing with a strong sense of confidence that people who do not and/or cannot know Jesus will at least have a chance to go to Heaven, our next chapter will tackle an even more debated and controversial question about who can go to Heaven and who cannot—those who have died without salvation!

CHAPTER XIII

Do the Dead Get A Second Chance To Go Heaven?

A re all people who die without salvation bound for Hell? What about those who had never heard about Jesus or His Gospel? What about those who did a lot of good things during their lives? Is there any chance for post-mortem repentance and acceptance of Jesus?

These are questions about a very divisive issue that many of us may have asked but likely never gotten answers for. So let's review the relative Bible verses for both sides, discuss what we read, and see what answers become apparent:

Verses That Disprove Post-Mortem Salvation?

Those who believe that there is no possibility of receiving salvation after death make no exceptions, no matter who it is that dies. That is, they believe it does not matter whether deceased people had done good works or bad works, or whether they had ever heard about Jesus or His Gospel. Nobody at all gets a post-mortem shot at Heaven.

Most people who take strong stands on Biblical issues have their favorite Bible verses handy to prove their points. Post-mortem salvation supporters and opponents are no different.

Let's first see the evidence of the opponents. One of their main pieces of evidence is the Biblical story about a rich man and a beggar named Lazarus in Luke 16:

> **Luke 16:22-26** (NIV)
>
> *"The time came when the beggar died and the angels carried him to Abraham's side. The rich man also died and was buried.*
>
> *In Hades, where he was in torment, he looked up and saw Abraham far away, with Lazarus by his side.*
>
> *So he called to him, 'Father Abraham, have pity on me and send Lazarus to dip the tip of his finger in water and cool my tongue, because I am in agony in this fire.'*
>
> *"But Abraham replied, 'Son, remember that in your lifetime you received your good things, while Lazarus received bad things, but now he is comforted here and you are in agony.*
>
> *And besides all this, between us and you a great chasm has been set in place, so that those who want to go from here to you cannot, nor can anyone cross over from there to us.'*

Does Luke 16 Really Disprove Post-Mortem Salvation?

According to those who say there is no post-mortem salvation, the main point in these verses is at the end where Luke says that a great chasm divides Hades from Heaven and that no one can cross to the other side. They say this means no salvation for those in Hades.

So from that perspective, this seems to be a compelling argument against post-mortem salvation, because the rich man is indeed in Hades and cannot go to the Heavenly place where Lazarus is.

Or Does Luke 16 Actually Prove Post-Mortem Salvation?

From another perspective, however, Luke 16 may actually turn out to be a compelling argument *for* post-mortem salvation. That is, it may actually support the idea that people can receive salvation after they die.

What do I mean? It all starts with the definition of *Hades*. Many people, including most post-mortem salvation naysayers, believe that Hades is synonymous with Hell. Well, that's not quite true. In the New Testament, Hades is an entirely different word and concept. Hades, from the Greek word Ἅιδης, is the *temporary* place or realm of the dead as they await final judgement. It is not the final place where souls go after the final judgement. The final unpleasant place is Hell, not Hades. By the way, Hades, in most instances, is a direct translation of the Hebrew word Sheol—לִשְׁאֹל, which also means temporary realm or place of the dead.

Do We All Go to Hades/Sheol?

Yes, Hades, as described in the New Testament, is the general place where all souls—good and bad— temporarily go after physical death.

Two Separate Regions in Hades/Sheol?

Do I mean that all souls are together in the very same place after physical death? No. What I mean is that, although all souls go to a general place called Hades (or Sheol), that general area is divided into two distinct regions that separate some souls from others. One region is a pleasant Heavenly area for those who did enough good things.

This pleasant region of Hades was most likely the *Paradise* or *third heaven* that Paul described during his out-of-body trip.

The other region of Hades is an unpleasant area for those who didn't do enough good things in life. As proof of these two regions of Hades, we need look no further than—you guessed it—Luke 16!

Verse 22 says that the beggar Lazarus went to Abraham's side (Actually Abraham's bosom from the Greek word κόλπον—kolpon), which was the pleasant part of Hades. The Heavenly area, again, is Paradise— from the Greek word παράδεισος (paradeisos).

The rich man went to the deepest and most unpleasant area of Hades, which is called *Tartarus*, from the Greek word Τάρταρος (tartaros). Incidentally, the Bible says those in Tartaros are also in prison or in chains (2 Peter 2:4).

Spirits Confined Inside the Earth?

Even though Tartarus is a region deep in the earth, it is a spiritual place. Spirits cannot be imprisoned by physical conditions on or below the earth, so those conditions have to be spiritual in nature. It is somewhat analogous to spirits who linger in areas on the surface of the earth where we live. They are among us, but cannot be restrained by us, because we are physical and they are spiritual.

What about Spirits/Ghosts Still Roaming the Earth?

Let's divert our attention for just a short while from our main topic of Paradise and Tartarus to briefly address the fact that not all spirits/ghosts permanently remain in the afterlife/Hades region that we are discussing.

I'm sure we've all asked ourselves at some point why some spirits/ghosts are not in Hades and are allowed to remain on earth among the living. Mark 5 tells us about many of them:

> **Mark 5: 8, 12, 13** (NIV)
>
> *For Jesus had said to him, "Come out of this man, you impure spirit!"*
>
> *The demons begged Jesus, "Send us among the pigs; allow us to go into them."*
>
> *He gave them permission, and the impure spirits came out and went into the pigs. The herd, about two thousand in number, rushed down the steep bank into the lake and were drowned.*

Many Spirits/Ghosts Among Us Are Demons?

Yes. These verses clearly tell us that the spirits who came out of this man and then possessed the pigs were demons (aka unclean/impure spirits) who numbered in the thousands. And if this many spirits were able to possess one man, just imagine how many total demons might be among us.

Given the presence of so many demons/unclean spirits, it is entirely possible that many ghosts, and in some cases poltergeists, that we might see, hear, or even feel are demons. After all, what do they do when they are not possessing someone? And those situations do occur as we can see in the following verse:

Matthew 12:43 (NIV)

When an impure spirit comes out of a person, it goes through arid places seeking rest and does not find it.

I think it is very possible that a restless demon could be noisy and mischievous.

What About the Other Spirits/Ghosts Among Us?

Other spirits/ghosts that we might see or hear who are not demons are mainly either angels who are here to help us or other spirits who are here for special purposes. The following verses tell us about angels:

Hebrews 1:14 (NIV)

Are not all angels ministering spirits sent to serve those who will inherit salvation?

Hebrews 13:2 (NIV)

Do not forget to show hospitality to strangers, for by so doing some people have shown hospitality to angels without knowing it.

Other Spirits/Ghosts

Other spirits/ghosts that appear among us include the spirits of dead people. The following is an example of this:

1 Samuel 28:13-15 (NIV)

...The woman replied to Saul, "I have seen a divine being coming up from the ground!"

He said to her, "What about his appearance?" She said, "An old man is coming up! He is wrapped in a robe!"

Then Saul realized it was Samuel, and he bowed his face toward the ground and kneeled down. 15 Samuel said to Saul, "Why have you disturbed me by bringing me up?"...

In these verses, we see the spirit of a man of God, Samuel, who had died and gone to Paradise, and had now been summoned by a medium on behalf of King Saul, who was having severe problems in his kingdom. We can see here that even though God generally frowns on mediumship (Leviticus 19:31, Deuteronomy 18:11,...), it does work, meaning the spirits of dead people can be summoned, and we can sometimes perceive them through one or more of our senses.

Interestingly enough, the Bible does not mention a limit on how long the spirits of the deceased can remain among us after they are summoned. It also does not address whether the spirits of the deceased can appear to us in ways other than mediumship.

Summary of Spirits/Ghosts on Earth

So, to summarize this short section, the Bible indicates that, generally speaking, the spirits/ghosts that appear on earth are either demons, angels, or perhaps spirits of the deceased. There may be times when it is unclear what type of spirit is present or why it is present.

Back to Paradise and Tartarus

Okay, let's return to our main section on the division of Hades into Paradise and Tartarus; namely, verses that confirm this division:

Confirmation that Hades/Sheol is Divided into Paradise and Tartarus?

There are a number of verses that confirm that Hades/Sheol is divided into two areas, pleasant and unpleasant:

> **Luke 23:43** (NIV)
>
> *Then he said, "Jesus, remember me when you come into your kingdom.*
>
> *Jesus answered him, "Truly I tell you, <u>today you will be with me in paradise."</u>*

Here Jesus tells the thief on the cross beside Him that the thief would be in Paradise with Him, meaning the paradise section of Hades/Sheol.

> **2 Peter 2:4** (HCSB)
>
> *For if God didn't spare the angels who sinned but threw them down into Tartarus and delivered them to be kept in chains of darkness until judgment;*

This verse tells us that sinful angels were sent to Tartarus, the negative hellish part of Hades/Sheol where they would remain as prisoners until the final judgement.

I'm sure it's evident that I didn't use the NIV version of this verse. That's because the NIV version translates the Greek word

Τάρταρος (Tartaros) as Hell, which is misleading to say the least. Yes, Tartarus is a type of Hell, but it is a temporary place in the deepest part of Hades/Sheol where all bad souls (like the sinful angels) are imprisoned until the final judgement. Hell is the place where they go after the final judgement.

Jonah 2: 2, 4, 6 (WEB)

He said, "I called because of my affliction to Yahweh. He answered me. Out of the belly of Sheol I cried. You heard my voice.

I said, 'I have been banished from your sight; yet I will look again toward your holy temple.'

I went down to the bottoms of the mountains. The earth barred me in forever: yet have you brought up my life from the pit, Yahweh my God.

Important Reasons Why We Know Jonah Went to Tartarus:

These verses say in very clear terms that Jonah went to Tartarus for the following reasons:

1. We know he went to Hades, because he names Sheol as the place he went to.
2. He begged God to release him from a very low place in the earth ('bottoms of the mountains' and 'the pit'), which was a common description of Tartarus' location.
3. Jonah says in verse 6 that he was "barred...in..." in that low region of the earth. Being imprisoned in Sheol/Hades is a common experience for those in the Tartarus region.

4. In verse 4, Jonah indicates that he was separated from God, which is the number one indicator of the hellish condition of spiritual death. We'll return to this topic in later chapters.

Did Jonah Really Die Inside the Whale?

Yes, by all Biblical indications he did. Jonah disobeyed God's clear order to go to Nineveh. Deliberately disobeying God is one of the worst sins that we can commit, and immediately puts us into disfavor with God and creates a strong reason for Him to punish us in some way.

God punished Jonah by arranging for him to have the above-mentioned NDE in Tartarus. By going to Tartarus, Jonah experienced the 'affliction' of separation from God, and begged God for mercy. He was released only after acknowledging his disobedience and repenting.

Psalm 88:3 (ISV)

For my life is filled with troubles as I approach Sheol.

This is King David telling us that he is on his way to Sheol/Hades as his death approaches. Surely if David, a man of God, is going to Sheol/Hades, it means he is going to the Paradise region and not Tartarus, right? Of course. So Psalm 88:3 is a clear example of the fact that Paradise is a part of Sheol/Hades.

Again, I chose not to use the NIV version of this verse because of a misleading translation of an important word; in this case, the word *Sheol*. NIV translated Sheol as death, which is actually a mistranslation. The word for death in Hebrew is תוומ (mavet), which is an entirely different concept. Sheol is the name of a place, and that is the place or realm of the dead.

So, from one perspective, it appears that Luke 16 disproves post-mortem salvation, but from another perspective it seems to prove it. What do you think? Many of us can probably already see my position on this. I'll make it clearer a little later.

Moving on, let's now examine another verse that post-mortem salvation naysayers say disproves post-mortem salvation: Hebrews 9:27:

Does Hebrews 9:27 Disprove or Prove Post-Mortem Salvation?

Hebrews 9:27 (NIV)

Just as people are destined to die once, and after that to face judgement,

According to those who believe there is no post-mortem salvation, the fact that verse 27 says that we are judged after we die means that the judgement is final and that, therefore, there is no chance for repentance, salvation, or anything else other than being sent to our final destination of either Heaven or Hell.

On the one hand, if we focus superficially on just the wording of this one verse, it seems to disprove post-mortem salvation.

On the other hand, if we look below the surface at the semantics and at the verse's entire context, we can see this verse differently. This is because post-mortem salvation naysayers are assuming that 1) the "judgement" spoken of is the final judgement, and 2) omitting the rest of the context in verse 28 is inconsequential.

So with these issues in mind, let's now examine both verses together:

Hebrews 9:27, 28 (NIV):

Just as people are destined to die once, and after that to face judgment, so Christ was sacrificed once to take away the sins of many; <u>and he will appear a second time, not to bear sin, but to bring salvation to those who are waiting for him</u>.

Is it the First or the Final Judgement?

First of all, we know that right after we die, we go to one of the two regions in Sheol/Hades to await final judgement, right? So the judgement in verse 27 cannot be the final judgement.

Also, before we are assigned to one of the regions in Sheol/Hades, we have to be evaluated, aka judged by God in order to determine whether we go to Paradise or Tartarus, right?

That means that verse 27 is referring to the first judgement that we receive after dying, which is the one that determines which part of Sheol/Hades we are assigned to.

Do We Have to Wait for Salvation?

Second, verse 28 says that Christ will appear a second time to bring salvation to those waiting on Him. But who are those who are waiting on Him to bring salvation? And why are they waiting? According to Jesus in all of the Gospel books, His sacrifice made salvation available to everyone—immediately—and is given to anyone who repents, believes in Jesus, and accepts Him as their personal savior (John 3:16).

So, theoretically, we could receive salvation in less than five minutes, meaning that no waiting is necessary.

So Who Has to Wait for Salvation?

Again, since Christ's instructions on how to receive immediate salvation were aimed at flesh-and-blood people like us, this means that no living people have to wait for salvation, because we can receive it instantly by sincerely repenting, believing in Jesus, and accepting Him as our personal savior.

So if flesh-and-blood people are not the ones waiting for salvation, who is waiting? Well, there are only two types of souls that need salvation—those with physical bodies and those without. Those without physical bodies are normally those who are in Sheol/Hades, where many souls went before Christ brought salvation to the world. It, therefore, refers those souls who are awaiting the salvation that Christ will bring.

So, Hebrews 9:27 *does not* disprove post-mortem salvation, but actually provides strong support *for* it!

Let's now review another verse that, at first glance, appears to disprove post-mortem salvation even more convincingly than the previous two verses — 2 Corinthians 5:10:

2 Corinthians 5:10 (NIV)

For we must all appear before the judgment seat of Christ, so that each of us may receive what is due us for the things done while in the body, whether good or bad.

This verse clearly states that we will be judged on the things we do while in our living physical bodies.

Does 2 Corinthians 5:10 refer to just the final judgement, which would preclude repentance and salvation after physical death?

No, not at all. Let's examine another verse that will add important context to 2 Corinthians 5:10 and tell us what it really means:

> **Acts 10:42** (NIV)
>
> *He commanded us to preach to the people and to testify <u>that he is the one whom God appointed as judge of the living and the dead</u>.*

This verse states that God appointed Jesus Christ as the judge of the living and the dead. By referring to the judgement of both the living and the dead, this verse clearly means that there are two different judgements: 1) His judgement of the living is judgement of what we do in our physical bodies and 2) His judgement of the dead can only mean His judgement of what we do in Sheol/Hades to determine our final destination.

Let's now turn to the other side of the question—what Biblical evidence do the supporters of post-mortem salvation have?

Verses That Prove Post-Mortem Salvation?

Those who believe we can receive salvation after we die also have certain verses that they use to prove their view. Let's examine a few of them to see if we agree, and I strongly believe the first one will more than set the tone for the rest:

> **1 Peter 3:18-20** (WEB)
>
> *Because Christ also suffered for sins once, the righteous for the unrighteous, that he might bring you to God; being put to death in the flesh, but made alive in the spirit; in which <u>he also went and preached to the spirits in prison, who before were disobedient</u>,*

when God waited patiently in the days of Noah, while the ship was being built. In it, few, that is, eight souls, were saved through water.

Wow! I think the verses we just read justified that exclamation. Why? There are a number of reasons:

1. <u>No Interpretation Needed</u>--These are among the very few verses that we've reviewed thus far that have not needed to be interpreted in a certain way. These are crystal clear in their main message (especially verse 19 and part of 20) that, after Jesus' resurrection from the dead, He went down into Hades and preached to spirits there.

2. <u>Jesus Preached in Tartarus</u>-- He preached to those in the lowest part, the Tartarus section of Hades. We know this because the verses say these spirits were in prison, and, as we learned earlier, Tartarus is the place in Hades where spirits are imprisoned (2 Peter 2:4).

3. <u>Jesus Gave Them Post-Mortem Salvation!</u>—He preached to and saved imprisoned spirits who had been disobedient to God when they were flesh-and-blood people. This shows in the clearest possible terms that post-mortem salvation was given to those spirits.

4. <u>2 Corinthians 5:10 Does Not Disprove Post-Mortem Salvation</u>-By saying that Jesus provided post-mortem salvation to those spirits in Tartarus, this verse confirms that the judgement of the "living and the dead" in 2 Corinthians 5:10 above was actually two different judgments—the first one right after we die to determine what part of Hades we go to, and the second one after we go Hades to determine whether we go to Heaven or Hell.

Translation Issue

As you've probably noticed again, this is another verse where I chose not to use the NIV version. It's because the NIV translated the Greek word ἐκήρυξεν (ekeiryxen) as 'proclaimed' instead of 'preached.' While it's true that 'proclaimed' and 'preached' are used synonymously in many New Testament verses, the NIV itself normally translates it as 'preached' (for example, see the NIV translations of this word in Matthew 3:1, Mark 14:9, and 1 Corinthians 1:23, to name a few).

Generally, I choose the version based two main factors: 1) How closely it sticks to the original Greek (or Hebrew in the Old Testament) and 2) how clear the style is. In most cases, I choose NIV, because it meets these criteria better than most others. But not always. I believe this is the third time, thus far that I've chosen another version over NIV, and I'm sure it won't be the last.

More Verses that Prove Post-Mortem Salvation?

While 1 Peter 3:18-20 was a strong tone-setter for this section, other verses seem capable of continuing that tone quite convincingly:

Psalm 86:13 NKJV

For great is Your mercy toward me, And You have delivered my soul from the depths of Sheol.

Another NIV Translation Issue

I chose the NKJV over NIV because of more translation issues:

In Psalm 86:13, NIV translated the original Hebrew שְׁאוֹל (Sheol) as simply death, which is not true. The Hebrew word for death is another word: מוות (mavet).

The NKJV kept *Sheol* as simply *Sheol*, which is correct, because we know what *Sheol* is without having to interpret it to something that means something else.

Also NIV translated the Hebrew חַסְדְּךָ (chesedcha) as "your love," which is also wrong. חַסְדְּךָ means your mercy (or your grace), as the NKJV translated it.

> **Ephesians 4:7-9** (NASB)
>
> *But to each one of us <u>grace was given</u> according to the measure of Christ's gift.*
>
> *Therefore it says, "<u>When He ascended on high, He led captive the captives</u>, And He gave gifts to people."*
>
> *(Now this expression, "He ascended," what does it mean except that <u>He also had descended into the lower parts of the earth</u>?*
>
> *He who descended is Himself also He who ascended far above all the heavens, so that He might fill all things.)*

As Convincing as 1 Peter 3:18-20?

From at least one perspective, Ephesians 4 is just as convincing, if not more so, as 1 Peter 3 as evidence in support of post-mortem salvation. And here's why:

Ephesians 4 has all the main points of 1 Peter 3; that is:

- Christ descends into Tartarus ("the lower regions of the earth") and helps the imprisoned spirits ("captivity") there.

- The verse also names Christ's grace as the preface to His leading the captives out of Tartarus and giving "gifts" to people.
- The grace in 1 Peter 3 is seen in the fact that Jesus preached to the imprisoned spirits. And what would be the point of preaching to the spirits if the possibility of grace was not involved. So both sets of verses dovetail perfectly with each other.

Yet Another NIV Translation Problem

No sooner had I pointed out the previous two NIV translation problems, than another one reared its ugly head with Ephesians 4.

The problem with Ephesians 4 is NIV's translation of the Greek phrase "καὶ κατέβη εἰς τα κατώτερα μέρη τῆς γῆς" (kai katebe eis ta katotera mere tes ges).

For some reason, NIV translated this phrase as "he also descended to the lower, earthly regions," which means essentially that Jesus descended to regions that were lower than Heaven, and those lower regions included the earth. This misses the point entirely, which the NASB translation captures perfectly:

The NASB translation of this phrase is much better because it is identical to the literal translation directly from the Greek, which is "He also descended into the lower regions of the earth." In other words, He did not descend into lower regions that included the earth, but into lower regions inside the earth itself.

And, of course, it is this direct translation from the Greek that tells us that Jesus descended into Tartarus and led prisoners out.

The next verse seems even more supportive of post-mortem salvation:

1 Peter 4: 4-6 (NIV)

They are surprised that you do not join them <u>in their</u> <u>reckless, wild living</u>, and they heap abuse on you.

But <u>they will have to give account to him who is ready</u> <u>to judge the living and the dead.</u>

For this is the reason the gospel was preached even to <u>those who are now dead</u>, so that they might be <u>judged</u> <u>according to human standards</u> in regard to the body, but <u>live according to God in regard to the spirit.</u>

Strong Evidence of Post-Mortem Salvation?

These verses also deserve an exclamation mark! They give extremely strong evidence of post-mortem salvation:

- First Jesus judges the living. Peter even tells us some of the human vices that He considers when He judges them.
- Then He preaches the Gospel to the dead, to give them the same opportunity for salvation as the living have.
- Then He judges the dead using the same standards that He uses with the living. That is, even though they are no longer in physical bodies, the spirits are held accountable for the same types of vices and rewarded for the same types of merits as physical people would be.

<u>Final Thoughts on Post-Mortem Salvation</u>

For those of us who have participated in our discussions, post-mortem salvation is no longer an unsettled controversy. It is now a settled Biblical fact. We know this from verses that state not only that spirits in Tartarus have gotten chances to receive salvation, but also that Christ Jesus actually took trips there for that very purpose.

As relates to us now, no one knows for sure what our fate will be after we pass from this life. But there's one thing we can control after we die. When we're judged right after this life, we can make sure Jesus notices at least one consistently good quality in our behavior—namely that we really tried to live a good spiritual life!

Briefly Back to the NDE Trips to Heaven and Hell—Were They To Paradise and Tartarus?

At the end of Part II, we said that we would briefly return to the topic of the NDE trips to Heaven and Hell for further clarification. Well, this chapter provides that clarification. First, we now know that right after we die, we go to places that we generally associate with either Heaven or Hell. Those places are Paradise and Tartarus.

Second, we know that the NDE trips to Heaven and Hell were to those places. That is, the NDE trips to "Heaven" were to Paradise, which is the upper region of Hades, while the trips to "Hell" were to Tartarus, which is the lower region.

This is a perfect segue to another earlier question that we can now answer—Was the rich man really burning in Hell?

Was the Rich Man Really Burning in Hell?

Regarding the rich man's experience of fire in Tartarus, it was both a form of punishment and a way to make him see the error of his ways on earth.

The rich man is obviously experiencing some form of unpleasantness, since he mentions flames and wanting water to cool his tongue. But it's also clear that he is not engulfed in the hellfire that most of us imagine about Hell.

There are several reasons why we know that the rich man was not really engulfed in a sea of flames:

- The rich man basically just wanted Lazarus to bring him a little drop of water to cool his tongue. If he were really burning in a pit of raging fire, he wouldn't just be thinking about cooling his overheated tongue. The pain everywhere would be unbearable.

- Why would the rich man even think that Lazarus could bring him the water unless he knew that Lazarus would not experience the same unpleasant heat that the rich man was experiencing? Surely he knew that Lazarus would not willingly walk into a pit of fire.

- In Abraham's answer to the rich man, he said that that spirits on the Paradise side could not go over to the Tartarus side, because they could not cross the chasm between them. He said nothing about Paradise spirits having to walk through fire.

- The rich man sounded too calm, clear-headed, and rational to be in the agony that he would experience if he were really roasting in fire.

- The Bible tells us that Tartarus is a place of darkness and imprisonment, not fire (2 Peter 2:4). Thus, any form of pain or discomfort other than darkness and imprisonment would be tailor made for specific spirits, not for all of them. In other words, this temporary Hell is experienced by different souls in different ways according to their sins (Revelation 22:12, Romans 2:6).

- Given the above-mentioned points, and noting that the rich man specifically complained about an overheated tongue, what he most likely experienced was some painful but limited form of heat that he noticed more in his tongue than anywhere else. It was painful enough to make him beg for mercy, but mild enough so that he could still maintain his composure and think about the things that he had done wrong in life.

Post-Mortem Salvation for the Rich Man?

Quite possibly. The rich man sounds very contrite and humble, addressing Abraham as "Father Abraham" and asking for pity. Showing qualities like remorsefulness, humility, and reverence to Abraham clearly indicates that the rich man was well on his way to repenting and improving himself spiritually.

Another Controversial Topic?

For further clarification on why fire is associated with Hell, please continue to the next chapter—is Hell really a place of eternal fire?

CHAPTER XIV

Is Hell Really an Eternal Fire?

Many of us have undoubtedly grimaced at the unsettling thought that after we die our souls might be sent to some immense underground cavern filled with raging fire and pungent sulfur to remain there forever, always awake and in agony, while we're literally roasting every single moment with no chance of ever getting relief or getting out.

This horrifying picture of Hell is so unnerving that many people have undoubtedly sought salvation more out of their desire to avoid Hell than their desire to go to Heaven.

But does the Bible actually say that Hell consists of never-ending burning? We'll answer that question shortly.

Is Hell Called *Gehenna* in the Bible?

Indeed it is. There is no Greek word for Hell in the New Testament that sounds like Hell, but the place that we call Hell and associate with fire and brimstone is usually called *Gehenna* in the Bible. At times, more descriptive words like fire, furnace of fire, and 'never-ending fire' are used, but in the majority of cases, it is *Gehenna*.

Gehenna is the English transliteration of the Greek word γέεννα (nearly the same pronunciation), which comes from the Hebrew word גֵּיא הִינוֹם (Ge Hinnom), which means 'Valley of Hinnom.' It is also called גיא בן הינום (Ge Ben Hinnom), which means 'Valley of Hinnom's Son.'

Is *Gehenna* a **Real Place?**

Absolutely. As we can see in the images below, *Gehenna* (*Ge-Hinnom*) is a real place to the south of Jerusalem that still exists today. It used to be a garbage dump in ancient times where fire was always kept burning in order to consume the waste and reduce the foul odors.

Thus, when the Bible speaks of the eternal fire of Hell, it often uses *Gehenna*, which is a direct reference to the perpetual fire of *Ge-Hinnom* where there was (in Biblical times), for all intents and purposes, eternal fire and eternal destruction (of waste), as we see in the following verses:

Matthew 10:28 (NIV)

Do not be afraid of those who kill the body but cannot kill the soul. Rather, be afraid of the One who can destroy both soul and body in hell.

In this verse, "Hell" is translation from *Gehenna*. And the verse says souls are "destroyed" there.

And even in the few instances where *Gehenna* per se is not used, the imagery is still "*Gehenna*-like" in that it still refers to a never-ending fire scenario. For example:

Matthew 25:41 (NIV)

Then he will say to those on his left, 'Depart from me, you who are cursed, into the eternal fire prepared for the devil and his angels.

This verse uses the Greek word for fire πῦρ (pir) in the phrase πῦρ τοò αἰώνιον (pir to aionion). Aionion is normally translated as 'eternal,' but has the additional meaning of 'of the ages.' So the phrase can literally mean either 'eternal fire' or 'fire of the ages.'

To round out the common image of Hell as eternal fire, let's see a couple more well-known hellfire verses:

Matthew 5:22 (NIV)

But I tell you that anyone who is angry with a brother or sister will be subject to judgment. Again, anyone who says to a brother or sister, 'Raca, is answerable to the court. And anyone who says, 'You fool!' will be in danger of the fire of hell.

Jude 1:7 (NIV)

In a similar way, Sodom and Gomorrah and the surrounding towns gave themselves up to sexual immorality and perversion. They serve as an example of those who suffer the punishment of eternal fire.

So Is Hellfire Real or Symbolic of Something Else?

These verses certainly give us the strong impression that Hell is really eternal torment in never-ending fire, don't they? In my many discussions on this topic, however, I sometimes hear a question that entertains another possible interpretation—is hellfire actually a symbol for something else?

Well, it just so happens that the people who posed that question were thinking along the same lines as I was. You see, I believe that *Gehenna* and other words for hellfire are indeed symbols for something else. And that something else is a very important part of a frequently recurring Biblical theme—death and destruction!

Are Death and Destruction Different?

Death and destruction may sound like two completely different words, but in the ways most important to our discussion, they are the same. Of course, in earthly physical terms, the Law of Conservation of Matter states that a physical thing cannot be destroyed in the sense of total annihilation so that absolutely nothing of it remains. But that is a theoretical concept that has no practical use or application in terms of human or spiritual experience or the Bible's use of the term.

In the ways most relevant to what we can perceive and comprehend as humans and spirits, and, most importantly, in the ways that the Bible uses the word, the concepts of death and destruction are virtually synonymous.

A quick example of this is in the Old Testament where Abishai is about to kill Saul so that Saul could no longer try to kill David, but David intervenes and spares Saul's life:

1 Samuel 26:9 (NIV)

But David said to Abishai, "Don't destroy him! Who can lay a hand on the Lord's anointed and be guiltless?

As we can see, instead of the word 'kill,' this verse uses the word "destroy" as a synonym for 'kill.'

"Destroy" here is a perfect translation of the Hebrew verb תחַשׁ (shachat), which literally means to damage, corrupt, or destroy. If the verse had used 'kill,' it would have been the Hebrew word גרָה (harag), which is the verb used in Genesis 3 where Cain kills Abel.

Biblically Speaking, What Are Death and Destruction?

In terms of human experience and Biblical usage, we can define both death and destruction in the same general manner—the removal of the external and internal qualities and conditions that are necessary to maintain the original identity and functions of an entity (living or non-living thing). Of course, the term 'death' is normally used only with living things; but otherwise, the two words are generally interchangeable, as we saw in 1 Samuel 26:9 above.

Thus, when a living thing, for example, a person dies, death destroys the external qualities and conditions (their appearance and structure deteriorate) and, most importantly, destroys the internal qualities and conditions (organ function ceases) that make life possible.

So, now that we all clear on what we mean by death and destruction, let's use it to look at eternal fire in a different light:

Replace Hellfire with Death in the Bible?

Exactly. Let's substitute death for hellfire in each of those verses above and see if my interpretation is plausible:

> **Matthew 5:22:** *But I tell you that anyone who is angry with a brother or sister will be subject to judgment. Again, anyone who says to a brother or sister, 'Raca,' is answerable to the court. And anyone who says, 'You fool!' will be in danger of the fire of hell.*

In this verse, *Gehenna* is used in the phrase γέενναν τοῦ πυρός (Geennan tou piros), which is usually translated as "fire of Hell." Literally, however, it means *'Gehenna* of fire' or 'fiery *Gehenna.'*

A Form of Death for Souls?

Using the imagery of the fire of *Gehenna* or *Ge-Hinnom* (the burning garbage dump) in this manner, the "fire of hell" could very well be a place that does to souls, in a manner of speaking, what *Ge-Hinnom* did to garbage.

That is, *Gehenna* could be a place where souls are deprived of *life*-giving qualities and conditions and subjected to some radical *life*-removing change, just as the garbage thrown into *Ge-Hinnom* was deprived of the *life* of its original qualities and changed into a new lifeless darker form (ashes).

In other words, just as the garbage of *Ge-Hinnom* was subjected to a form of death and destruction, souls could very well be subjected to the same. Please recall that a number of verses in this section specifically describe hellfire as "death" for souls.

But how can an immortal soul be sentenced to death? A great question. If there's one thing we already know, it's that a soul's death will not come through fire and brimstone, but through some other life-removing process. We'll discuss that process and offer an answer a little later. In the meantime, let's see if the remaining verses say the same thing about the death of a soul:

> **Matthew 10:28:** *Do not be afraid of those who kill the body but cannot kill the soul. Rather, be afraid of the One who can destroy both soul and body in hell.*

Here *Gehenna* is translated as 'Hell' in the phrase καὶ ψυχὴν καὶ σῶμα ἀπολέσαι (kai psychin kai soma apolesai en Geenne) ἐν γεέννῃ, which means 'destroy both souls and body in Hell.

First, please take note that the Bible uses the words "kill" and "destroy" as synonyms.

Second, this verse does not say that souls will be tormented in the fire of *Gehenna*, but rather that they will be "killed" or "destroyed." In other words, this verse also says that souls will *die* in Hell.

> **Jude 1:7**: *In a similar way, Sodom and Gomorrah and the surrounding towns gave themselves up to sexual immorality and perversion. They serve as an example of those who suffer the punishment of eternal fire.*

First, this verse tells us in very clear terms that the destruction of Sodom and Gomorrah was an example of the "eternal fire" that awaits those who disobey God.

This verse used the Greek term for eternal fire-- πυρός αἰωνίου (piros aioniou), but it obviously does not really mean that the destruction of Sodom and Gomorrah was "eternal" in the same way that we normally think of that word. After all, it occurred with a single divine act of destruction and ended in a relatively short period of time.

This means that, again, the Bible is not equating eternal fire with an actual place of eternal painful flames, but with a single act of death and destruction.

Verses that State Even More Clearly that Hell is Death?

After reviewing verses that state very clearly that Hell is death, is it possible that the Bible can be even clearer on this issue? It certainly seems that way, judging from the following verses on the "second death":

> **Revelation 20:14-15**: *Then death and Hades were thrown into the lake of fire. The lake of fire is the second death.*

Anyone whose name was not found written in the book of life was thrown into the lake of fire.

In these verses, death, Hades, and disobedient souls are all "thrown into the lake of fire." First of all, death is a state of being and Hades is a vast underground area, so disobedient souls are the only ones on this list that could actually be thrown anywhere.

So the only relevant interpretation of the "lake of fire" that could happen to a state of being, a place, and a soul would be death and destruction, right?

And it just so happens that the end of verse 14 tells us in the clearest possible manner that this "lake of fire" is actually death—the "second death!"

And the NIV translation is 100 percent accurate. The Greek phrase θάνατος ὁ δεύτερός (Thanatos ho deuteros) literally means "the second death."

> **Revelation 21:8:** *But the cowardly, the unbelieving, the vile, the murderers, the sexually immoral, those who practice magic arts, the idolaters and all liars— they will be consigned to the fiery lake of burning sulfur. This is the second death."*

This verse also tells us that sinners will be sent to a lake of fire and that this fate is the "second death."

The original Greek for the relevant phrase in this verse is actually τῇ λίμνῃ τῇ καιομένῃ πυρὶ καὶ θείῳ (te limne te kaiomene piri kai theio) which literally means "the lake of burning fire and sulfur." But "fiery lake of burning sulfur" works too.

The "second death" Thánatos is a perfect translation of the same Greek phrase used in Revelation 20:14 (ὁ Θάνατος ὁ δεύτερος — ho thanatos ho deuteros).

Conclusive Evidence that Eternal fire is Death?

In my opinion, these last two verses demonstrate conclusively, with no interpretation needed, that *Gehenna*, hellfire, eternal fire, and other references to punitive fire are symbols for spiritual death.

It shouldn't be a surprise to anyone that these references to *Gehenna*-like conditions mean spiritual death. Let's recall three important reasons why:

> The two verses above (and other earlier ones) clearly state that hellfire is death, death and destruction make

more contextual sense than an actual fire, and verses throughout the Bible, including some we've just read, tell us that the spiritual choices we make ultimately result in either eternal life or death.

What about 'Eternal'? -- Is It Always a Correct Translation?

On the one hand, we have all agreed that the fiery part of Hell in the phrase 'eternal fire' doesn't really exist but is a metaphorical name for spiritual death. But what about the 'eternal' part of that spiritual death? Why do translators use that word so often?

So, let's pose two relevant questions about 'eternal':

1. Is the word 'eternal' an accurate translation of the original Hebrew or Greek in every Bible verse in which 'eternal' appears?
2. If 'eternal' is not always an accurate translation, what should the translation be?

To address the first question, let's make sure we familiarize ourselves with the basic meaning of the Hebrew and Greek words that are translated as 'eternal':

Hebrew -- *Olam*

Currently, the Hebrew word עוֹלָם (olam) is translated as mainly 'world' and 'universe' (with some exceptions). But in earlier Old Testament days *olam* had mostly time-related meanings like age, eternity, 'distant past,' 'distant future,' and long period of time (in the past or future). Other forms of olam (le-olam, ad-olam, etc) had similar time-related meanings like eternal, and forever.

As a matter of fact, it may surprise many of us that olam appears over 400 times in the Old Testament and is translated almost exclusively as a time-related word there, and almost never as 'world' or 'universe.'

Greek – Aion

The Greek word αἰών (aion) basically means 'age' or 'eon,' and the different forms of its adjective αἰώνιος (aionios) similarly mean 'of an age/eon' or 'regarding an age/eon.'

In the Bible, *aion* is used as the Greek translation of *olam* and its variations. This is especially evident in the Septuagint, which is the Greek translation of the Old Testament, which was written almost entirely in Hebrew.

So let's very quickly review a few Bible verses in which forms of *olam* and *aion* appear and see if they are translated correctly:

> **Jonah 2:6** (NIV)
>
> *To the roots of the mountains I sank down; the earth beneath barred me in forever. But you, LORD my God, brought my life up from the pit.*

The "forever" here is the NIV translation of *olam/aion*.
The Hebrew word in this verse is לְעוֹלָם (le-olam)
The Greek word is αἰώνιοι (aionioi)

Conclusion: This is a mistranslation, and the reason is obvious: This is Jonah talking about his time inside the whale. And we know for a Biblical fact that Jonah was only in the whale for three days. Therefore it could not have been "forever," right?

Exodus 21:6 (NKJV)

Then his master shall bring him to the judges. He shall also bring him to the door, or to the doorpost, and his master shall pierce his ear with an awl; and he shall serve him forever.

This "forever" is also from *olam/aion.*

The Hebrew word again is לְעֹלָם (*le-olam*)

The Greek is εἰς τὸν αἰῶνα (eis ton aiona)

Conclusion: This is also a mistranslation, and the reason is clear: Slaves cannot serve their masters forever, because a person cannot physically live forever. Therefore, "forever" is absolutely false.

1 Chronicles 28:4 (NIV)

Yet the LORD, the God of Israel, chose me from my whole family to be king over Israel forever. He chose Judah as leader, and from the tribe of Judah he chose my family, and from my father's sons he was pleased to make me king over all Israel.

The *olam/aion* word here is "forever."

The Hebrew is לְעוֹלָם

The Greek is εἰς τὸν αἰῶνα (eis ton aiona)

Conclusion: Another mistranslation, and for the same reason as in Exodus 21:6. No matter how strong or holy a king is, as long as he is a flesh-and-blood human, he cannot physically live forever. So again, a correct translation would be 'until death' or 'until the end of my life.'

Answer to the First Question

I think we've read enough verses to enable us to answer the first question, and I think the answer is pretty obvious: No, 'eternal' is not always correct when it appears as a translation of the words *olam* and *aion*. The word 'eternal' in these verses is clearly out of place.

Answer to the Second Question—Spiritual, Death, Destruction?

After giving it a lot of thought and research, I believe that when we see verses where 'eternal' is not a correct translation, we should substitute one of the following terms if the context allows it: 'spiritual,' 'death,' or 'destruction,' or similar terms like 'destructive', 'until death,' or 'end of life,' whichever fits the context.

But please don't take this as an <u>eeny</u>, meeny, miney, moe selection method. The terms 'spiritual,' 'death,' and 'destruction,' are all closely related—each one implies the other:

Spiritual, Death, and Destruction are Closely Related?

Absolutely. And to remove or drastically reduce any doubts we might have about my answer to the second question, please consider the following points:

1. Our physical bodies are temporary, meaning that they last for only about 100 years, give or take a few, right? But our spirits are the permanent part of us, meaning that we are spiritually 'eternal,' right?

2. In order for flesh-and-blood people to become our 'eternal' selves, meaning spirits, our physical bodies have to experience what? Yes, death. And let's recall that, for Biblical purposes, 'destruction' is a synonym of 'death.'

3. The part of us that receives a reward or punishment after physical death is what? Right again, our 'eternal' part.

4. Lastly, and perhaps most importantly, these terms (spiritual, death, and destruction) are all components of the recurring themes of spiritual life and death both on earth and in the afterlife.

So 'Eternal' Refers to the Non-Physical?

Exactly. To summarize my point, in many Bible verses, the word 'eternal' does not refer to how long an entity (living or non-living) will last, but rather to the non-physical or the end-of-physical state that an entity is in or is headed to. And that state is the 'eternal' part of us—our spirit.

For people, it is the death or destruction of our physical bodies that brings us to our 'eternal' spiritual state.

While we have this thought in mind, let's quickly review some of the verses above and substitute a form of 'spiritual,' 'death,' or 'destruction' where 'eternal' does not work, and see if the substitution makes sense:

Jonah 2:6 (NIV)

To the roots of the mountains I sank down; the earth beneath barred me in <u>forever</u>. But you, LORD my God, brought my life up from the pit.

"Forever" ('eternally') does not work here as a translation of Hebrew לְעֹלָם (le-olam) and Greek αἰώνιοι (aionioi). But will a form of one of the three substitution terms work? In my opinion, yes. And that term is 'spiritually'.

So let's read Jonah 2:6 again and replace 'forever' with 'spiritually':

To the roots of the mountains I sank down; the earth beneath barred me in (spiritually). But you, LORD my God, brought my life up from the pit.

I'm sure we all recall why 'spiritually' works here, right? To refresh our minds, it's for the following reasons:

- Our first stop after physical death is the afterlife (Hades)
- The afterlife is divided into Paradise and Tartarus.
- Tartarus is often referred to as a 'pit' and a 'prison' (with bars) that imprisons spirits.
- Both ideas ('pit' and 'bars') appear in this verse, meaning Jonah's spirit is imprisoned in Tartarus for a while.

So, I'm sure it's now clear that 'spiritually' is contextually appropriate and correct as a translation of לְעֹלָם (le-olam) and αἰώνιοι (aionioi) and that 'forever' is incorrect.

Exodus 21:6 (NKJV)

Then his master shall bring him to the judges. He shall also bring him to the door, or to the doorpost, and his master shall pierce his ear with an awl; and he shall serve him forever.

Again, "forever" ('eternally') does not work as a translation of Hebrew לְעֹלָם (le-olam) and Greek αἰῶνα (aiona) in this verse. So let's substitute a form of 'death' ('until death' or 'until the end of life') and see what happens:

Then his master shall bring him to the judges. He shall also bring him to the door, or to the doorpost, and his master shall pierce his ear with an awl; and he shall serve him (until death/until the end of life).

I think it's clear that this form of 'death' is the correct translation of לְעֹלָם (le-olam) and αἰῶνα (aiona) in this verse. After all, what is the maximum time the servant could serve his master in this physical life? Exactly—until death or until the end of the servant's life. Certainly not 'forever.'

1 Chronicles 28:4 (NIV)

Yet the LORD, the God of Israel, chose me from my whole family to be king over Israel <u>forever</u>. He chose Judah as leader, and from the tribe of Judah he chose my family, and from my father's sons he was pleased to make me king over all Israel.

"Forever" ('eternally') is definitely out of place as a translation of Hebrew לְעֹלָם (le-olam) and Greek εἰς ὁ αἰῶνα (eis ho aiona) in this verse. No mortal king can reign forever. So let's substitute a form of 'death' ('until death' or 'until the end of life') and see if it fits:

Yet the LORD, the God of Israel, chose me from my whole family to be king over Israel <u>(until death/until the end of life)</u>. He chose Judah as leader, and from the tribe of Judah he chose my family, and from my father's sons he was pleased to make me king over all Israel.

I think it's obvious that this form of 'death' is the correct translation of םָלֹעְלַ (le-olam) and εἰς ὁ αἰῶνα (eis ho aiona) in this verse. A human king can only serve until the end of his life, right. Definitely not 'forever.'

Jude 1:7 (NIV)

In a similar way, Sodom and Gomorrah and the surrounding towns gave themselves up to sexual

immorality and perversion. They serve as an example
of those who suffer the punishment of <u>eternal fire</u>.

Let's now connect Jude 1:7 with the following verse:

Ezekiel 16:53 (NIV)

However, I will restore the fortunes of Sodom…

I think we can all immediately see how inappropriate 'eternal' fire is in Jude 1:7. I think a more appropriate translation of πυρὸς αἰωνίου (piros aioniou) is death/destruction and here's why:

First of all, and most importantly, we see that Ezekiel 16:53 tells us that the punishment wasn't "eternal," because Sodom's fortunes were to be restored later.

Second, it is certainly more appropriate to think of what happened to Sodom and Gomorrah as a single act of 'death/destruction' than an 'eternal' fire.

And even if the verse was referring to the people in Sodom and Gomorrah, they did not suffer an 'eternal' fire either. Again, it was a single act of death/destruction that undoubtedly sent them to Tartarus.

I think I'll end our examples here to avoid monotony. But they hopefully sufficed to clarify my point.

'Eternal' Not Always Wrong?

Am I saying that 'eternal' is always incorrect as a Biblical translation? Not at all. Just as it's very obvious when it's incorrect, as in the verses above, it's also very obvious, in most cases, when it's correct.

For example, 'eternal' is perfectly correct for describing things that obviously last forever, especially when referring to things like divine attributes. The following verse is an illustration:

Ephesians 3:21 (NIV)

To him be glory in the church and in Christ Jesus throughout all generations, for ever and ever! Amen.

According to the original Greek, the time being referenced is τοῦ αἰῶνος τῶν αἰώνων (tou aionos ton aionon), which literally means 'the age of the ages.'

But this is talking about the glory of God—a divine attribute. And since we know without a doubt that God's attributes are eternal, we can translate the original Greek as 'eternally' or "forever and ever," because we know it's true.

What About Eternal Fire During NDEs?

Hopefully it's clear to us that the hellfire seen during the NDEs was simply what we've been discussing in this chapter—-symbols of the spiritual death these men could have received had they not changed the spiritual course of their lives.

The horrifying thought of being trapped in a blazing fire pit forever is undoubtedly a way to frighten sinners into rethinking their behavior. The punishment they would really receive—spiritual death—would also torment them, but in other ways.

Does 'Eternal' Death in Hell Last Forever?

Good question. We'll provide an answer for that in the next chapter where we'll also discuss 'eternal' life in Heaven in more detail.

CHAPTER XV

Heaven and Hell–Eternal Life and Death After Final Judgement?

If hellfire and Hell are spiritual death, it stands to reason that Heaven is the exact opposite--spiritual life—right?

While we're here on earth as physical people we gain spiritual life through salvation or spiritual death through evil. And as we know, this spiritual life that we receive through salvation is also called 'eternal' life (John 3:16).

However, while we're physically alive, such 'eternal' life is not really eternal in the sense of lasting forever, because, as we know from earlier discussions, we can lose our salvation if we don't continue our belief in Christ or at least regain it before we die.

Then after we physically die, our spiritual life or death will gain us entry into either the Paradise or Tartarus levels of the afterlife (Hades).

After the final judgement, our spiritual (or 'eternal') life or death becomes synonymous with our final destination of either Heaven or Hell.

Before we focus exclusively on Heaven and Hell, let's briefly explore the Biblical theme of life versus death a little more for the following two reasons:

1. Our entire existence--current and future--and our final destination in Heaven or Hell depend on the spiritual life-and-death decisions we make.

2. The Bible places enormous importance on this theme by the sheer number of verses on it, making it one of the most frequently recurring themes in the Bible.

Eternal Life vs. Death a Recurring Biblical Theme?

Many verses throughout the Bible tell us that good spiritual choices lead to eternal life and bad choices lead to eternal death. The Bible emphasizes this theme particularly regarding our "eternal" destinies after the final judgement. Here are a few of them:

Jeremiah 21:8 (NIV)

You shall also say to this people, 'Thus says the Lord, Behold, I set before you the way of life and the way of death.'

Romans 7:9 (NIV)

I was once alive apart from the Law; but when the commandment came, sin became alive and I died;

John 3:16 (NIV)

For God so loved the world, that he gave his only Son, that whoever believes in him should not perish but have eternal life.

John 5:24 (NIV)

Truly, truly, I say to you, he who hears My word, and believes Him who sent Me, has eternal life, and does not come into judgment, but has passed out of death into life.

Romans 5:21 (NIV)

So that, as sin reigned in death, grace also might reign through righteousness leading to eternal life through Jesus Christ our Lord.

John 10:28 (NIV)

I give them eternal life, and they will never perish, and no one will snatch them out of my hand.

Ok, now that we've allowed the Biblical importance of this theme to sink in a little deeper, let's discuss those destinies a little more in the context of what they actually are—Heaven and Hell:

What Are Heaven and Hell?

As physical beings on earth, we are in a limited state of spiritual life, joy, peace, love, and righteousness when we are, in a manner of speaking, "with" God, through the salvation provided by His Son, Jesus Christ. By the same token, we are in a state of spiritual death and separation from God if we intentionally commit evil actions in deliberate disobedience of God.

It follows, therefore, that the spiritual (eternal) life, joy, peace, love, and righteousness that we call Heaven is also being with God, but in a direct and full sense of the idea. And the spiritual death that we call Hell is being literally cut off from God in the fullest sense of the term.

Being in Heaven is Being with God?

While we're physically alive, our fleshly bodies, with all their emotional and instinctive distractions, naturally limit the extent to which we can be with God, because God is pure spirit.

When we leave our bodies and become souls or spirits, we are closer to His full reality, closer to His plane of existence and, therefore, can be with Him more fully. If we are with God in Heaven, we are completely with Him. The places where we are spiritually in His presence are Paradise before the final judgement and Heaven afterwards. Both are places of spiritual bliss.

Hell is Being Without God?

People on earth who deliberately commit acts that they know are evil are spiritually dead, but can still have what they might consider positive experiences like financial success and pleasure by focusing on their physical sides.

As spirits, however, the spiritually dead are completely separate from God and have no physical life from which to derive anything positive. They, therefore, experience only negativity with nothing positive to look forward to. No order, only chaos, Only deeply disturbing and emotionally painful feelings. We know this because the Bible tells us that these are souls who will not be where Abraham is (recall that Abraham was in Paradise when the rich man was in Tartarus):

Luke 13:28 (NIV)

There will be weeping there, and gnashing of teeth, when you see Abraham, Isaac and Jacob and all the prophets in the kingdom of God, but you yourselves thrown out.

The operative phrase in this verse, of course is "weeping and gnashing of teeth," and it is a perfect translation of the original Greek: ὁ κλαυθμὸς καὶ ὁ βρυγμὸς τῶν ὀδόντων (ho klauthmos kai ho brigmos ton odonton). This verse indicates that souls in Hell (temporarily in Tartarus or after the final judgement) will be outside of the presence of God, which will cause extreme discomfort.

Also think about the affliction felt by the rich man and Jonah when they went to Tartarus which, again, is a form of Hell. And recall the hellish horror experienced by two men in the chapters on NDEs. These are also examples of what happens during spiritual death, which is separation from God.

So The Second Death is Also Hell?

Yes, the second death is the Hell, i.e., the spiritual death— separation from God— that sinners experience after the final judgement.

The following verse explicitly tells us that life with God is Heaven and life without Him is Hell:

2 Thessalonians 1:9 (NIV)

They will suffer the punishment of eternal destruction, away from the presence of the Lord and from the glory of his might,

Where are Heaven and Hell?

The only thing we can be absolutely sure about regarding the location of Heaven is that it is the spiritual place where we go after the final judgement where we have spiritual life and intensely positive experiences like peace, joy, love, and righteousness in God's full presence.

The exact location of Heaven, however, is irrelevant. To use an analogy, when we think of Air Force One, we normally think of the modified 747 that the President normally uses. However, any airplane that the President uses becomes Air Force One. The common denominator among them all is the President's presence. By the same token, wherever we experience God's full presence is Heaven.

On the other hand, Hell's location is the spiritual place where souls go after the final judgement where there is only spiritual death and where souls have intensely negative experiences. Again, the exact location is irrelevant, but wherever it is, the defining factors of that location are spiritual death and total separation from God.

Does Eternal Life in Heaven Last Forever?

Well, I think we can safely say yes. Since Heaven and the souls who inhabit Heaven are spiritual and eternal, the souls can remain there for eternity, or an unlimited amount of time.

One tiny qualification is that even in Heaven souls retain their free will to leave or stay. But who would want to leave the peace, love, joy, righteousness, and divine presence that we would experience in Heaven? I'm quite sure that there will never be another Lucifer there.

Does Eternal Death in Hell Last Forever?

The answer to this question is yes, and no. And for a reason similar to why I said souls 'can' instead of 'will' remain in Heaven forever—because souls have a free and changeable will.

So, yes, souls condemned to Hell at the final judgement will indeed remain there forever—if they don't change their minds. On the other hand, if they do change, i.e. renew, their minds, they can possibly leave.

I think I can hear many of us saying 'What in the world is this guy talking about?' And before we get too confused over this, let's digress a little in order to get some background information that will hopefully help clarify my point:

The 'Eternal Fire' of *Gehenna*?

Let's recall the Bible's use of *Gehenna* (from the Hebrew גיא הינום (Ge Hinnom—Valley of Hinnom), for its eternal hellfire imagery. Earlier, we established that the eternal fire of Hell was actually spiritual death. So *Gehenna* is one of the Bible's images of eternal spiritual death or, again, Hell:

Revelation 20:14 (NIV)

Then death and Hades were thrown into the lake of fire. The lake of fire is the second death.

As we discussed earlier, the *second death* is also another name for Hell, because it's after the first death (leading to Tartarus) and after the final judgement. And, of course, after the final judgement, there will be no further spiritual need for death and Hades (more specifically Tartarus), so both will be sent to the *lake of fire,* which, again, is Hell.

But why does the Bible specifically use the fire in *Gehenna* as the chosen image for Hell? I think the answer lies in *Gehenna's* original purpose:

Gehenna was a place (garbage dump) used for the process of eventually changing filthy, toxic, maggot-ridden, foul-smelling garbage to a different non-offensive form by burning away its offensive qualities.

Gehenna then became the Bible's metaphorical way to convey the same idea spiritually— that the "eternal fire" of spiritual death could eventually "burn away" toxic spiritual qualities and bring about a positive change in an evil soul.

In other words, just as the garbage of *Ge-Hinnom* was subjected to a form of death and destruction that eventually changed it to a non-offensive form, souls could very well be subjected to the same transformation through an agonizing experience of spiritual death.

Since, as we learned in the previous chapter, the form of spiritual death in temporary Hell (Tartarus) varies according to the individual soul's sins, it stands to reason that the form of spiritual death in Hell will also vary according to the individual. (Revelation 20:12, 13; 1 Peter 4: 5, 6...)

So, the process of (individualized) spiritual death could eventually bring an evil soul to the point of spiritual transformation through genuine acknowledgement of and repentance for past sins, and a genuine change of heart and mind regarding good and evil. If this happens, the tormenting eternal fire of spiritual death would no longer be necessary for that soul.

The Kingdom of God?

Now that we've reached the end of our discussion on the eternal life and death that we receive in Heaven and Hell, we have one more question to pose about the nature of Heaven—is Heaven the same as the Kingdom of God?

CHAPTER XVI

Is Heaven the Same as the Kingdom of God?

This chapter will be a big change from the previous few in two ways. First, it won't be nearly as long, because the question of whether Heaven is the same as the Kingdom of God (also called the Kingdom of Heaven) will be much easier to answer. Second, the verses we will review need no re-translation and, therefore, much less discussion and reinterpretation.

After we review the verses, we'll be more than ready to answer two additional questions—what is the Kingdom of God? How does it differ from Heaven? First, however, let's answer the chapter question:

The Chapter Question and Answer

So, is Heaven the same as the Kingdom of God? The answer: No. They're very close, but not exactly the same.

The Reason?

Why aren't they exactly the same? Let me illustrate the reason why with another question: Is a car the same as a vehicle with wheels?

Our first thought might be yes, because these two things are also very close to each other in meaning. So close, in fact, that if we ask 'is a car always a vehicle with wheels?' the answer would be yes.

But what if we ask 'is a vehicle with wheels always a car? Then we'd have to say no, because there are many other kinds of vehicles with wheels that are not cars. So all cars are vehicles with wheels, but not all vehicles with wheels are cars.

In other words, in order to say that A = B, we'd also have to be able to say B = A, which we cannot say with cars (A) and vehicles with wheels (B), right?

For the very same reason, we cannot say that Heaven = the Kingdom of God. That is, while all of Heaven is in the Kingdom of God, not all of the Kingdom of God is in Heaven.

In other words, the Kingdom of God is to Heaven, what vehicles with wheels are to cars. To summarize the answer, the Kingdom of God includes Heaven and other things as well.

The Biblical Proof?

How do I know that the Kingdom of God includes more than Heaven? How about the first two verses of the Lord's Prayer?:

> **Matthew 6: 9, 10** (NIV)
> *This, then, is how you should pray:*
> *Our Father in heaven, hallowed be your name,*
> *Your kingdom come, your will be done, on earth as*
> *it is in heaven.*

This verse tells us in the clearest possible way that the Kingdom of God is present in both Heaven and earth.

Here are a few other verses about the Kingdom of God (also called Kingdom of Heaven). While reviewing them, let's try to get a feel for what that Kingdom is and then try to answer those two additional questions afterwards:

Other Bible Verses about the Kingdom of God

Psalm 45:6 (NIV)

Your throne, O God, will last for ever and ever; a scepter of justice will be the scepter of your kingdom.

Psalm 103:19 (NIV)

The Lord has established his throne in heaven, and his kingdom rules over all.

Daniel 7:18 (NIV)

But the holy people of the Most High will receive the kingdom and will possess it forever—yes, for ever and ever.'

Matthew 12:28 (NIV)

But if it is by the Spirit of God that I drive out demons, then the kingdom of God has come upon you.

John 3:3 (NIV)

Jesus answered him, "Truly, truly, I say to you, unless one is born again he cannot see the kingdom of God."

Luke 17:20-21(NIV)

Once, on being asked by the Pharisees when the kingdom of God would come, Jesus replied, "The coming of <u>the kingdom of God is not something that can be observed,</u>

Nor will people say, 'Here it is,' or 'There it is,' because <u>the kingdom of God is in your midst."</u>

1 Corinthians 4:20 (NIV)

For the kingdom of God does not consist in talk but in power.

Romans 14:17 (NIV)

For the kingdom of God is not a matter of eating and drinking, but of righteousness, peace and joy in the Holy Spirit,

So What is the Kingdom of God? How Does it Differ from Heaven?

From the verses we just reviewed, I think a few things are obvious about the Kingdom of God:

It is the spiritual life, the peace, the love, the joy, and the righteousness that emanates from God's presence and through His grace for those who submit to His rule. For us, this is mainly through salvation. (John 3:3)

It is not confined to any one place, but extends to wherever God's presence is. (Luke 17:20-21)

Flesh-and-blood people on earth can feel it and be empowered by it, but in a more limited way than spirits in Heaven. (Romans 14:17, 1 Corinthians 4:20)

The Difference?

As we know from previous chapters, Heaven is also the spiritual life, peace, love, joy, and righteousness we receive in God's presence. The main difference is that we can enjoy the Kingdom of God now as physical people, but we cannot reach Heaven fully until after we pass on into eternity.

Part IV

Now that we're finished with our discussions about Heaven and Hell, I'm sure at least some of us have the following question in mind--does that mean we're fresh out of interesting Bible controversies? Absolutely not! On the contrary, some of us may think the ones we'll tackle in Part IV are the most controversial ones in the entire book. So let's read on and decide for ourselves.

PART IV

Other Questions about Christianity

CHAPTER XVII

Female Authority over Men and Female Leadership in Church–Is It Biblical?

Many of us have heard people claim that the Bible teaches that women should always be submissive and should not have authority over men or be leaders in church.

Are those people correct? To put it bluntly, no. After a lot of reading and reviewing, I've found that the Bible actually teaches the opposite—that women can indeed have both authority over men and leadership roles in church.

People who generalize and say the Bible teaches against women having authority over men and leadership in church may not realize it, but they are mostly referring not to the Bible as a whole, but to one single source in the Bible—the Apostle Paul.

Our Purpose and Focus

I will demonstrate and highlight in the following sections and verses that Paul's instructions against female authority and leadership were almost never direct orders from God. Instead they were nearly always either indirectly inspired guidelines or optional recommendations or a combination of both.

In addition, Paul's instructions were never meant as a remedy for all problems involving all women in all churches in all situations, but for particular problems involving particular women in particular churches in particular situations. And even in those specific situations, his guidelines were strongly marked by his personal views and preferences.

As a result, Paul's instructions, for the most part, boiled down to guidelines with limited and often optional applicability for both the direct recipients of his instructions and for others in other situations. Paul himself highlights this fact by his inconsistent application of these guidelines. You see, Paul sometimes praised women who were in positions of authority and leadership!

So we will focus mainly on the limited and optional nature of Paul's instructions, but we will also review verses that show that the Bible as a whole does not teach against female authority and leadership. Together, these facts will help us to more clearly understand why Paul's guidelines should not have been applied to all women in his day and certainly should not be applied to women today.

Main Verse against Female Authority and Church Leadership?

Let's first check the verse cited most often as evidence that the Bible teaches against female authority over men and female leadership roles in church. It is part of Paul's instructions on how prayer and church services should be carried out:

1 Timothy 2:12 (NIV)

I do not permit a woman to teach or to assume authority over a man; she must be quiet.

This verse certainly seems to ring with a tone of clarity, finality, and certainty in its apparent message that women should not have authority over men and should not have a position of leadership in church. This would mean, among other things that a women could not tell a man what to do in any situation and could not be a teacher in church. But does the Bible really say that?

Context is of Paramount Importance

Understanding the words in a message without understanding the context is a recipe for not only misunderstanding the message but also for misrepresenting it when we tell others. That is, if we don't understand the background information on why something happened, we can easily say something about it that is completely false.

For example, there might be a police report that includes a section that says that a driver who was turning right hit a child who was walking across the zebra crossing at that corner at the same time. If we read just this section of the report, our initial impression would probably be that the driver wasn't paying attention to pedestrians in the zebra crossing and, therefore, was at fault.

But if we read the rest of the report, we will find out that the driver had actually stopped at the zebra crossing as the child was walking, but his car was rear-ended by another car and driven into the child.

Thus, our initial impression of that isolated section was completely false. Why? Because the context gave that section a completely different meaning.

Does the Context Surrounding 1 Timothy 2:12 Change Anything?

Indeed it does, and the context follows:

Background

First of all, Paul wrote the entire book of 1 Timothy to the Apostle Timothy, an evangelist who often accompanied Paul on his missions. Timothy became the leader of the church in Ephesus and was having trouble unifying everyone under the same doctrine and preventing the teaching of false and heretical doctrines.

Paul's Purpose for Writing 1 Timothy

Paul's main purpose for writing 1 Timothy was to offer a type of cook-book advice narrowly focused on helping Timothy to get everyone on the same doctrinal page, and 1 Timothy 2:12 was part of this attempt. Paul's purpose and reason for writing 1 Timothy is summarized in these two verses that he wrote:

> **1 Timothy 1:3, 4** (NIV)
>
> *As I urged you when I went into Macedonia, stay there in Ephesus so that you may command certain people not to teach false doctrines any longer, or to devote themselves to myths and endless genealogies. Such things promote controversial speculations rather than advancing God's work—which is by faith.*

Reasons for These Instructions

But why did Paul choose these particular instructions? He gave these instructions as a kind of extreme reaction against what he considered extreme conditions among Christians there. He was especially appalled at the teaching of false and pagan doctrines. So he felt that an urgent situation called for an urgent remedy.

It's clear that Paul's urgent remedy was influenced to some degree by the patriarchal society of his day and his personal issues with women (which we will review shortly), but he sincerely believed that his instructions would help in the churches that were going through disunity and doctrinal difficulties.

Paul's purpose and reasons for writing his instructions notwithstanding, a very important part of the instructions that he himself acknowledged was that they were not orders from God but rather limited and sometimes optional guidelines.

Paul's Instructions Had Limited Applicability?

Yes. In other words, Paul's instructions were not direct divine orders that the church in Ephesus had to carry out, but rather indirect divine options that Paul presented in order to remedy the church's particular problems at that time and at that place. That is, Paul used directions that God had already given him regarding his own situation and adapted them in a manner that he personally thought would fit the situations of other people.

Let's have a quick look at some of the verses accompanying 1 Timothy 2:12 to understand the context even better:

1 Timothy 2: 8-12 (NIV)

Therefore I want the men everywhere to pray, lifting up holy hands without anger or disputing.

I also want the women to dress modestly, with decency and propriety, adorning themselves, not with elaborate hairstyles or gold or pearls or expensive clothes, but with good deeds, appropriate for women who profess to worship God.

A woman should learn in quietness and full submission.

I do not permit a woman to teach or to assume authority over a man; she must be quiet.

The Context in These Verses Shows the Following:

First of all, in most of the verses before verse 12, Paul starts off by saying "...*I* want...," meaning that these are *his* personal preferences.

In verse 11, Paul suggests that women be quiet and submissive, but he does not actually say a woman "*should* learn," as we see in the NIV translation. Instead he uses the Greek word μανθανέτω (manthaneto), which means 'let learn.' So the verse actually says 'let a woman learn," which means that Paul's suggestion is not as strong and insistent as the NIV translation indicates. This increases the optional nature of his guidelines.

Paul does not say *God* wants them to do these things or that the instructions are necessary for salvation.

Even in verse 12, Paul says "*I* do not permit," which, again implies his own preference and not God's.

The optional nature of Paul's guidelines means they are not always applicable. That is, they cannot be used in every situation, so they have limited applicability and would be questionable in other situations. We can see this even more clearly in other verses in 1 Timothy 2:

More Limited Applicability in 1 Timothy 2?

Indeed. Reviewing the last few verses in 1 Timothy 2, starting with verse 11, we can see more of how limited the applicability of Paul's guidelines is.

This is especially evident when we see the justification that Paul uses for his guidelines. We will review his justification after these verses:

1 Timothy 2: 11-15 (NIV)

11 A woman should learn in quietness and full submission.

I do not permit a woman to teach or to assume authority over a man; she must be quiet.

13 For Adam was formed first, then Eve.

And Adam was not the one deceived; it was the woman who was deceived and became a sinner.

15 But women will be saved through childbearing—if they continue in faith, love and holiness with propriety.

Does Verse 11 Set the Tone for the Rest of the Chapter?

Yes it does set the tone for the rest of the chapter; namely that women should be quiet, submissive, and second to men in authority.

Verse 12 results from verse 11 because submissive women cannot teach or assume authority over a man.

Paul's Justification—Not Supported by Scriptures?

In Verses 13 and 14, Paul justifies his comments on women's submissive behavior and subordination to men by saying women should be submissive because Eve was created after Adam and was the one who was deceived.

If verses 13 and 14 were Paul's sincere opinion, it was definitely a mistake, because the Scriptures do not support that opinion. Although the Scriptures say Eve was created as a suitable helper for Adam and that she was deceived, they don't say in any way that she is Adam's subordinate. As a matter of fact, the Bible indicates that they were equals:

Genesis 1: 27, 28 (NIV)

So God created mankind in his own image, in the image of God he created them; male and female he created them.

God blessed them and said to them, "Be fruitful and increase in number; fill the earth and subdue it. Rule over the fish in the sea and the birds in the sky and over every living creature that moves on the ground."

Gender Equality?

No question. To understand this better, let's turn to the original Hebrew: First, אֱלֹהִים בָּרָא אֶת הָאָדָם בְּצַלְמוֹ (Elohim bara et ha Adam betsalmo). This literally means God created *the Adam* in His image. And *the Adam* here does not mean the man named Adam. It means all of mankind, women and men, were created in His image. Equally. The last part of the verse confirms this ונקבה זכר אותם ברא (Bara otam zachar unekevah). This literally means "male and female he created them," as the NIV translation above indicates.

So these verses are referring to men and women equally. And God blesses both of them equally and tells both of them—not just the man—to rule over the earth.

Genesis 2: 23, 24 (NIV)

The man said, "This is now bone of my bones and flesh of my flesh; she shall be called 'woman,' for she was taken out of man."

That is why a man leaves his father and mother and is united to his wife, and they become one flesh.

Did Adam Also Acknowledge Gender Equality?

Absolutely. That's why Adam calls Eve "bone of my bones and flesh of my flesh." To confirm this, verse 24 reiterates that men and women become one flesh, meaning two halves (50 + 50) become one whole (100).

Even More Limited or Questionable Applicability in Verse 15?

Precisely. 1 Timothy 2:15 undoubtedly has the most questionable applicability in that entire chapter. It literally tells Timothy, directly and bluntly, that women can obtain salvation through childbearing!

This idea of Paul's is perhaps the most extreme result of his instructions for women to be submissive. He is saying, in effect, that if women willingly accept their submissive and subordinate roles by doing 'female' things like having babies, then this attitude will gain them salvation.

Did Paul Really Say "Salvation" Through Childbearing?

No question. He really said that. Some Bible scholars have suggested that Paul didn't mean women would receive "salvation," but that the Greek word he used meant something else, including that women would 'recover,' or be 'restored,' from some of the sinfulness that Eve created in the Garden of Eden, or that they would 'retake' or 'regain' some of their respectfulness through their children.

I think we can all agree that these are very questionable alternative translations.

The Original Greek Proves Them Wrong

Questionable and unacceptable. Those scholars have it dead wrong. The Greek word σωθήσεται (sothesetai) means saved in the sense of deliverance or receiving salvation and being redeemed from sins.

Greeks used other words for those other alternatives. For example the word for 'retake' is ξαναπαίρνω (xanapairno), 'regain' is ανακτώ (anakto), and 'recuperate' is αναρρώνω (anarrono). But, again, they used σωθήσεται (sothesetai) for being saved in the sense of deliverance or receiving salvation.

So, with instructions like these, it's no wonder that a number of Paul's guidelines have very questionable and limited applicability in many situations.

In other words, these guidelines may have had some applicability as part of Paul's instructions to the church in Ephesus, but are not necessarily what he could recommend in other situations.

An Even Clearer Example of Paul's Optional Instructions?

Are there verses elsewhere that make it even clearer than 1 Timothy 2 that Paul's instructions regarding women's roles in church and authority vis-à-vis men are optional guidelines?

Believe it or not, there are. It just so happens that we have a set of verses that many of us are familiar with where Paul makes the optional nature of some of his instructions crystal clear. These are recommendations to the Corinthians regarding the issue of marriage and sex:

1 Corinthians 7: 1-2, 6-9 (NIV)

1)...It is good for a man not to have sexual relations with a woman.

But since sexual immorality is occurring, each man should have sexual relations with his own wife, and each woman with her own husband.

6) I say this as a concession, not as a command.

I wish that all of you were as I am. But each of you has your own gift from God; one has this gift, another has that.

8) Now to the unmarried and the widows I say: It is good for them to stay unmarried, as I do. But if they cannot control themselves, they should marry, for it is better to marry than to burn with passion.

1 Corinthians 7 Is Full of Optional Instructions

These verses in 1 Corinthians 7 are prime examples of instructions with limited applicability:

- First of all, Paul stresses that these instructions were based on earlier advice that God had provided to him for his particular situation vis-à-vis women. Then Paul took those divinely based instructions and adapted them to the situation in Corinth—as optional guidelines.

- In verses 1 and 8, Paul stresses that they are just his own personal advice and not divine orders.
- In verse 7, Paul makes it clear that this advice was originally God's advice to him, which he then passed on to the Corinthians—as optional instructions.
- In verse 6, Paul says in the most direct terms possible that these instructions are not divine orders but rather optional guidelines.

So Take Paul's Optional Instructions with a Grain of Salt?

In certain cases, I would say yes. In some situations like 1 Corinthians 7, it goes without saying that Paul's guidelines regarding sex and marriage are not for everybody, especially today. But he apparently thought they were appropriate for the Corinthians during his time.

That's not to say that his advice was not divinely inspired. As we've already mentioned several times, his advice, or at least some version of it, was indeed divinely inspired, but often for him personally and not necessarily for all the recipients of his instructions.

More of Paul's Optional Instructions?

To illustrate the sheer number of cases where Paul gave optional guidelines to churches, let's review his instructions to the Corinthians regarding the covering of men's and women's heads and women's hair length. And note that he exhorts them to follow *his* personal advice, not the advice of Christ:

1 Corinthians 11: 1-7, 13, 14, 16 (NIV)

Follow my example, as I follow the example of Christ.

2 I praise you for remembering me in everything and for holding to the traditions just as I passed them on to you.

3 But I want you to realize that the head of every man is Christ, and the head of the woman is man, and the head of Christ is God.

Every man who prays or prophesies with his head covered dishonors his head.

5 But every woman who prays or prophesies with her head uncovered dishonors her head—it is the same as having her head shaved.

For if a woman does not cover her head, she might as well have her hair cut off; but if it is a disgrace for a woman to have her hair cut off or her head shaved, then she should cover her head.

7 A man ought not to cover his head, since he is the image and glory of God; but woman is the glory of man.

13 Judge for yourselves: Is it proper for a woman to pray to God with her head uncovered?

14 Does not the very nature of things teach you that if a man has long hair, it is a disgrace to him,

16 If anyone wants to be contentious about this, we have no other practice—nor do the churches of God.

Paul's Instructions in 1 Corinthians 11 Show Personal Preferences

Paul is clearly urging the church in Corinth to follow *his* personal example, not Jesus'.

Second, Paul gives advice on hair length and head covering. But his reasons are not related to salvation or God's will, but rather to what he believes are 'natural' reasons. He says it's "…the very nature of things…"

Third, Paul's instructions are also culturally influenced. We can see this in verse 2 where he references the "traditions" that he is adhering to.

Finally, these types of guidelines would make no sense in today's churches, because they would be culturally inappropriate and, again, have nothing to do with salvation.

What about Paul's Claim that His Instructions Were God's Will?

Excellent question. For most of this chapter, we've been noting that Paul's instructions, especially about female submissiveness, were not direct orders from God. But in 1 Corinthians 14, he actually does seem to strongly imply at one point that his remarks came directly from God:

1 Corinthians 14: 34, 37 (NIV)

Women should remain silent in the churches. They are not allowed to speak, but must be in submission, as the law says.

If anyone thinks they are a prophet or otherwise gifted by the Spirit, let them acknowledge that what I am writing to you is the Lord's command.

Does Paul Contradict Himself in the Same Chapter?

Yes, he most assuredly does contradict his own instructions for women to be silent. Consider the following verses earlier in the same chapter:

1 Corinthians 14: 26-28 (NIV)

What then shall we say, brothers and sisters? When you come together, each of you has a hymn, or a word of instruction, a revelation, a tongue or an interpretation. Everything must be done so that the church may be built up.

If anyone speaks in a tongue, two—or at the most three—should speak, one at a time, and someone must interpret.

If there is no interpreter, the speaker should keep quiet in the church and speak to himself and to God.

In verse 26, to whom is Paul speaking? Exactly. "…brothers and sisters." And what does he say to them? Right again. Without any gender differentiation, he says "each of you has a hymn, or a word of instruction…." He is clearly talking to both genders. But in verse 34, he falls back into his instructions for female submissiveness.

A Contradictory Exception

But such alleged connections between Paul's optional recommendations and divine will are more the exception than the rule. And remember, even with this one exception, Paul invalidates the alleged connection by contradicting himself.

Do Paul's Optional Instructions Invalidate 1 Timothy 2:12?

I would say no and yes. No, they don't invalidate 1 Timothy 2:12 (and 1 Corinthians 14: 34) if they only applied to the very limited situations in Ephesus and Corinth during Paul's lifetime, and if those guidelines really helped those churches.

But yes, they would indeed invalidate 1 Timothy 2:12 (and 1 Corinthians 14:34) if they are to be applied to other situations in the past, present, and likely the future.

Paul Also Shows a Different (Contradictory) Attitude Toward Women?

Absolutely. In other situations, Paul contradicts his instructions against female leaders on a massive scale. That is, he speaks glowingly about working with women who are church leaders and who have authority over men.

This difference in instructions regarding women underscores the optional, limited, and sometimes questionable applicability of some of his guidelines.

Examples of Paul's Approval of Women Leading Men

In a number of situations involving his ministry, Paul not only spoke of his approval of female church leaders, but he also happily worked with them in spreading Christianity:

1. In Acts 18, we see that Paul traveled with a woman named Priscilla and her husband Aquila for part of Paul's teaching trip to Corinth and Ephesus. In Ephesus, Priscilla co-taught a man named Apollos about the Gospel of Jesus:

Acts 18:26 (NIV)

....When Priscilla and Aquila heard him, they invited him to their home and explained to him the way of God more adequately.

Here, Priscilla is certainly teaching, clearly showing authority, and obviously not being silent.

In Romans 16, Paul is even clearer about Priscilla's role as a teacher. As a matter of fact, he introduces her as a "fellow worker in Christ Jesus," and the church services are at her house!

Romans 16:3, 5 (NIV)

Greet Priscilla and Aquila, my fellow workers in Christ Jesus.

Greet also the church that meets at their house.

A verse that makes it even clearer that Paul was not against women being figures of authority is also found in Romans 16:

Romans 16:7 (NIV)

Greet Andronicus and Junia, my fellow Jews who have been in prison with me. They are outstanding among the apostles, and they were in Christ before I was.

In this verse, Paul names Junia, a woman, as being one of the apostles. Surely, no one can qualify as an apostle if they cannot be vocal instructors of the Gospel, right?

Verses that are even more astounding in refuting the idea that Paul opposed women serving in church leadership roles can be found in the book of Philippians. In the fourth chapter, Paul talks about two women who are already church leaders!

Philippians 4:2, 3 (NIV)

I plead with Euodia and I plead with Syntyche to be of the same mind in the Lord.

Yes, and I ask you, my true companion, help these women since they have contended at my side in the cause of the gospel, along with Clement and the rest of my co-workers, whose names are in the book of life.

Your eyes do not deceive you. Paul is pleading with Euodia and Syntyche, both women, to come to an agreement in their church leadership roles. As we can recall, much of Paul's work involved improving church situations that had gone awry. Here is one where the two leaderships are obviously diverging too much in church doctrine.

Other Situations in the Bible Where God Has Used Women as Leaders

The following verses will show other situations in which God used women as leaders in Biblical days. We will also see that God did not require women to be silent, even in religious settings, and that He has sometimes allowed – even appointed – women to have authority over men.

Deborah

One such woman was Deborah, a prophetess in the Old Testament. The women and men in Israel came to her to judge their disputes:

> Judges 4:4-5 (NIV): .... *the Israelites went up to her to have their disputes decided She had political authority, and the people respected her decisions.*

Deborah also had religious authority and commanded soldiers in the name of God:

> Judges 4:6-8 (NIV): …. *She sent for Barak son of Abinoam from Kedesh in Naphtali and said to him, "The Lord, the God of Israel, commands you: 'Go, take with you ten thousand men of Naphtali and Zebulun and lead them up to Mount Tabor.*
>
> *7 I will lead Sisera, the commander of Jabin's army, with his chariots and his troops to the Kishon River and give him into your hands.'"*
>
> *8 Barak said to her, "If you go with me, I will go; but if you don't go with me, I won't go."*

Hulda

Hulda, another Old Testament prophetess provided strong religious leadership to a king and his men who needed help with a book:

> 2 Kings 22: 11-15 (NIV): *When the king heard the words of the Book of the Law, he tore his robes.*
>
> *He gave these orders to Hilkiah the priest...*"*Go and inquire of the Lord for me and for the people and for all Judah about what is written in this book that has been found...*
>
> *Hilkiah the priest.....went to speak to the prophet Huldah, who was the wife of Shallum ....She lived in Jerusalem, in the New Quarter.*
>
> *She said to them, "This is what the Lord, the God of Israel, says: Tell the man who sent you to me, 'This is what the Lord says: I am going to bring disaster on this place and its people, according to everything written in the book the king of Judah has read...."*

Nothing Really Unusual about Female Leaders?

Both Deborah and Hulda are prophets and women with authority and leadership over men. And nothing in the Scriptures even remotely indicates that there is anything unusual about these or any other female authority figures.

Conclusion

We noticed six main points regarding the ideas that women should be submissive and not have authority over men or leadership in church:

- It was not the Bible as a whole, but rather mainly the Apostle Paul that expressed such ideas.
- Paul's instructions were not direct orders from God for all recipients, but were sometimes divinely inspired guidelines for Paul's own life that Paul then modified and passed on to others in other situations.
- Because most of Paul's instructions contained elements of his own personal preferences and were mainly tailored for specific situations in specific places, they had limited and even optional applicability both for their intended recipients and, especially, for women and churches in other places and times.
- Paul's personal views against female authority and leadership were influenced by both the patriarchal society of those days and his personal issues with women.
- The fact that Paul praised some women in positions of authority and leadership highlighted the inconsistency and, therefore, the limited and optional nature of his instructions against women being in those positions.
- Finally, even though Biblical times were mostly patriarchal and most leaders were, therefore, male, women were sometimes called by God to be leaders, teachers, and authorities over men. And when they were, it was not seen as anything unusual. We saw numerous examples of this in the Old Testament and the New Testament.

Topics Getting More Controversial?

Although Biblical female leadership is one of our more controversial issues, it isn't the last one that we'll discuss. As a matter of fact, some of us might believe the last two chapters in this book are the most controversial of all, but we'll let you decide that. Meanwhile, it's time to tackle our penultimate controversy: did our souls exists before we were born?

CHAPTER XVIII

Pre-existence and Reincarnation—
Are They Biblical?

Did some conscious part of us—our soul or spirit—exist before we were physically born? And can our spirit incarnate more than once? Without a doubt these are two of the most controversial and avoided topics in the Christian world with believers in preexistence and reincarnation being a distinct minority.

When the Controversy Started

While it is still hotly debated today, the Christian controversy over the existence of the soul before birth actually began in the second and third centuries after Jesus' death, when early church father Origen of Alexandria was teaching his belief that God created our souls long before we began to incarnate and reincarnate. Some church leaders gradually began to see these teachings as threats to their doctrinal systems. The opposition grew until 553, centuries after Origen's death, when Emperor Justinian issued the so-called

"Fifteen Anathemas" against Origen's teachings, thus banning such ideas from the church.

Pre-existence

Most Christian churches today still oppose the idea of pre-existence, insisting that no part of us exists before birth and that our souls are created only after we have physical bodies. So let's first review some of what opponents say about pre-existence:

Opponents of Pre-existence

Many pre-existence naysayers will point to specific Bible verses that they say prove their point, including Genesis 2:7 (KJV):

> *And the LORD God formed man of the dust of the ground, and breathed into his nostrils the breath of life; and <u>man became a living soul</u>.*

At first glance, this sounds like convincing proof against pre-existence, because the verse says "and man became a living soul," which I underlined for emphasis. If correct, it means that our soul was created after our physical birth.

At second glance, however, it's not the proof that it seemed to be, and for a very important reason—a key word in this verse is mistranslated!

Mistranslation

Still owned and used by more people than any other translation, the King James Version of the Bible (and several other versions) incorrectly translates the original Hebrew phrase חיה נפש (*nefesh chaya*) as "living soul." This is incorrect. The correct translation is 'living being,' with *nefesh* meaning 'being' or 'creature.'

To illustrate the true meaning of *nefesh* in this verse, let's have a quick look at another verse in the same chapter—Genesis 2:19 (KJV):

> *And out of the ground the Lord God formed every beast of the field, and every fowl of the air; and brought them unto Adam to see what he would call them: and whatsoever Adam called every <u>living creature</u>, that was the name thereof.*

In the last line of this verse which is talking about animals that God created, I underlined "living creature." Guess what original Hebrew phrase this was translated from?

You're absolutely right –*nefesh chaya* (חיה נפש) *This* is the exact Hebrew phrase that the KJ version translated as "living soul" earlier in the same chapter!

The only translation that makes sense for both verses is 'living being' (or 'living creature'). And there are many instances in the Bible where *nefesh* means 'being' or 'creature,' but not 'soul.'

No Evidence Against Pre-existence?

Exactly. As we have just seen, this verse, correctly translated, says nothing against the idea that our souls existed before our bodies. It simply says that the physical being called man was created at that time.

Here is another type of verse that opponents of pre-existence see as evidence for their belief:

Psalm 139:13 (NIV)

For you created my inmost being; you knit me together in my mother's womb.

Pre-existence opponents apparently believe that this verse says that the "inmost being" here is our soul and that it was created with our bodies in our mother's womb.

If the "inmost being" is really the soul, then yes, this verse is strong evidence that pre-existence is false.

However, upon closer scrutiny, I discovered that the wording of this verse is misleading at best and completely incorrect at worst, which allowed a misinterpretation of the verse. In other words, there is a translation problem:

Another Mistranslation?

Yes indeed. After checking the original Hebrew, I found that we have the same type of translation problem with the NI version as we had with the KJ version of Genesis 2:7.

As most of us probably suspect, the incorrect part of this verse is the "inmost being." This phrase could be, and apparently is, being interpreted as the soul by those who reject the idea of pre-existence.

The Original Hebrew

The original Hebrew, however, is crystal clear in meaning and leaves absolutely no room for misinterpretation: כליותי (kilyotay) is the Hebrew word that was incorrectly translated as "my inmost being." But guess what this Hebrew word really means?

The literal translation of this Hebrew word is 'my kidneys!' That's right, 'kidneys.' This is so explicitly precise in meaning that the most we could fudge for stylistic reasons and still maintain reasonable accuracy is perhaps 'inner organs.' Translating it as "inmost being" goes much too far from the correct meaning.

Sticking closer to the Hebrew and translating כליותי (kilyotay) as 'my kidneys' or 'my inner organs' would also be consistent with the overall message of the verse, which is essentially that God used his omnipotence to form our physical bodies inside our mother's womb.

Does Hebrews 9:27 Disprove Biblical Reincarnation?

Hebrews 9:27 is invariably the main verse cited as Biblical proof against reincarnation. I know we're all familiar with this verse, because we discussed it in the chapter on post-mortem salvation. Normally we wouldn't repeat a topic, but since it's being used as evidence against our point in this chapter as well, we're obligated to discuss it again, at least briefly. But, it won't be a total repetition. Since we're discussing a different issue in this chapter, our comments about Hebrews 9:27 will differ accordingly:

> **Hebrews 9:27** (NIV)
>
> *Just as people are destined to die once, and after that to face judgment,*

Those who believe there is no reincarnation in the Bible, insist that Hebrews 9:27 disproves Biblical reincarnation in two ways: 1) it says we die once, and therefore, have only one incarnation and 2) it says after we die, we face final judgement, which would also mean no more incarnations.

Why Hebrews 9:27 Does Not Disprove Biblical Reincarnation

On the one hand, if we focus superficially just on the wording of this one verse, it does seem to disprove Biblical reincarnation.

On the other hand, however, if we look carefully at the meaning of key words and the verse's entire context, we will see that it doesn't disprove Biblical reincarnation at all.

We will see this after recognizing that Biblical reincarnation naysayers reached their erroneous opinion by: 1) misunderstanding the word "people," 2) by incorrectly believing that the "judgement" spoken of in this verse is the final judgement, and 3) by omitting verse 28, which provides half of the context of verse 27:

1) Who Are the "People" in this Verse?

To make sure we know who the "people" in this verse are and what's happening with them, let's turn briefly to the original Greek. The word ἀνθρώποις (anthropois) is a form of the Greek word for men or mankind. This means that 'people' is a perfectly good translation.

So now that we agree that the Greek word for 'people' is translated correctly, what's the problem with it? Where's the misunderstanding?

Hiding in Plain Sight?

Exactly. The misunderstanding of the word 'people' in this verse stems from the fact that it is there, but is being totally ignored!

Ignored? Absolutely. Why else would reincarnation naysayers insist that Hebrews 9:27 says that "we" only die once, when, in fact, this verse says that "people" only die once? What's the difference between "we" and "people?" A world of difference—literally.

Physical 'People' Only Live and Die Once

The last time I checked, 'people' are flesh-and-blood inhabitants of the physical world. And a flesh-and-blood person can live and die only once (even with NDEs, there is only one permanent death), right?

And we know from the chapter on post-mortem salvation that after 'people ' die, their souls are judged right afterwards and then go to one of the regions of the afterlife (Sheol/Hades).

It Is Our Souls, Not Bodies That Reincarnate?

Correct. 'People' live and die only once, because 'people' are physical entities subject to physical laws of nature. It is, therefore, only our souls that reincarnate, of course, not our bodies. And we are judged immediately after each incarnation as an assessment of how we lived that particular life and what spiritual issues and lessons we still have to work on.

But after each judgement, the soul can either remain in Sheol/Hades or, if it's in God's will, enter another incarnation.

So, again, in order to understand Hebrews 9:27 correctly, we must first be aware of the word "people" and put it in its proper perspective.

2) Is it the First or the Final Judgement?

The second thing we must do to correctly understand Hebrews 9:27 is to recall from the chapter on post-mortem salvation that the first thing that happens after the (one and only) death of a physical person is that the soul is judged and sent to one of the afterlife regions.

This means that verse 27 is not referring to the final judgement, but rather to the first one that we receive after physically dying.

3) The Context of Hebrews 9:27, 28 — Christ's Atonement for Our Sins?

Third, to understand Hebrews 9:27 correctly, we must also put it in its full context, which can be done only if we add verse 28:

> *Just as people are destined to die once, and after that to face judgment,*

So Christ was sacrificed once to take away the sins of
many; and he will appear a second time, not to bear sin,
but to bring salvation to those who are waiting for him.

When we read both verses together we can clearly see that the main point of Hebrews 9:27, 28 is not to inform us that people live and die only once, but rather to emphasize Christ's one-time atonement for our sins.

Something Everyone Should Know?

Precisely. If the fact that people live and die once were the main point, it would be like a verse telling us that people talk in order to communicate with each other or that people open their eyes in order to see. Of course it's true. It's self-evident and goes without saying.

It's also self-evident that people live and die only once and are then judged.

So, again, in order to emphasize Christ's one-time sacrifice to atone for our sins, Hebrews 9:27, 28 compares it to the one-time occurrence of something else that should be common knowledge to everyone; namely, the death and judgement of each (physical) person.

Okay, now that we've discussed and refuted the strongest evidence presented by those who deny Biblical pre-existence and reincarnation, let's next review some of the evidence of those who are convinced that the Bible does indeed teach these concepts:

Believers in the Pre-existence and Reincarnation of Souls

Those who believe in pre-existence and reincarnation say that we were souls long before we were born and that we incarnate from the afterlife into physical bodies, similar to how Jesus Christ, who pre-existed in Heaven, incarnated into a physical body as the son of Mary and Joseph.

The First Christian Believers in Pre-existence and Reincarnation?

Many of us might think that Christian belief in the existence of souls before birth started with Origen of Alexandria, whom we briefly discussed above. While it's true that the public controversy started with Origen, the belief itself did not. As a matter of fact the very first Christians to believe in pre-existence and reincarnation were also the very first Christians in world history—Jesus' own disciples!

Jesus' Own Disciples Prove Biblical Pre-Existence and Reincarnation?

I'm certain what I just said sounds unbelievable to many of us. So before we reject it as nonsense, let's review a Bible verse in John 9 that confirms it:

John 9: 1, 2 (NIV)

As he went along, he saw a man blind from birth. His disciples asked him, "Rabbi, who sinned, this man or his parents, that he was born blind?"

I'm fairly sure that anyone reading this verse, whether a believer or opponent of pre-existence and reincarnation, will agree that the disciples are indeed making reference to the pre-existence of the blind man. They're implying that he committed prior sins either as a spirit or in an earlier incarnation. And they're doing so in a very casual manner, as if there was nothing unusual about their question.

Although Jesus answers in verses 3-5 that neither the man nor his parents sinned to cause the blindness, He did not not invalidate the question. As a matter of fact, his answer confirms that it was a valid question:

John 9: 3,4 (NIV)

"Neither this man nor his parents sinned," said Jesus, "but this happened so that the works of God might be displayed in him. As long as it is day, we must do the works of him who sent me. Night is coming, when no one can work. While I am in the world, I am the light of the world."

Pre-Birth Sins Were Possible, But Not in This Case?

In other words, instead of saying that the man could not have sinned before birth or that pre-existence was impossible, Jesus said the man *did not* cause his blindness through pre-birth sins, which acknowledges the possibility that the man *could* have done so. Instead, according to Jesus, the man was born blind "so that the works of God might be displayed in him."

Jesus emphasized this point by saying that demonstrating God's power was part of His responsibilities during His incarnation, and healing the blind man was an opportunity to do so. He went on to say that he would continue to do such things because He was the light of the world for the duration of his incarnation.

But just in case some of us might not be convinced by what I said about John 9, let's look at another set of verses that seem to make it even more clear that sins before birth can affect an incarnation:

Clearer Verses that Pre-Birth Sins Can Affect an Incarnation?

In the following verses, Jesus demonstrates and articulates even more clearly than in John 9 that a person's pre-birth sins can affect that incarnation:

> **Matthew 9: 1-7** (NIV)
>
> ...Some men brought to him a paralyzed man, lying on a mat.
>
> When Jesus saw their faith, he said to the man, "Take heart, son; your sins are forgiven."
>
> At this, some of the teachers of the law said to themselves, "This fellow is blaspheming!"
>
> Knowing their thoughts, Jesus said, "....Which is easier: to say, 'Your sins are forgiven,' or to say, 'Get up and walk'?
>
> But I want you to know that the Son of Man has authority on earth to forgive sins." So he said to the paralyzed man, "Get up, take your mat and go home."
>
> Then the man got up and went home.....

These verses in Matthew 9 go one step farther than those in John 9 in their message that pre-birth sins can affect an incarnation. In John 9, the disciples wondered if pre-birth sins caused that man's blindness. In Matthew 9, Jesus emphatically confirmed that pre-birth sins caused the man's paralysis.

Then after saying that the man's pre-birth sins—either as a spirit or in an earlier incarnation—had caused his paralysis, Jesus then heals him by removing those prior sins.

Jesus Confirms Two Spiritual Truths

By setting up a crystal clear connection between the man's paralysis and his pre-birth sins and then healing him, Jesus underscores two important spiritual truths:

1. Souls exist before the physical bodies that they enter.
2. What souls do before an incarnation can and normally does affect that incarnation.

Let's have a quick look at two more verses that strongly support the reality of pre-existence:

Our Spirit *Returns* to God?

Ecclesiastes 12:7 (NIV)

And the dust returns to the ground it came from, and the spirit returns to God who gave it.

How could our spirits "return" to God unless they were there previously? Think about that for a second. If the verse was not referring to pre-existence, wouldn't it say something like the spirit would 'go' instead of 'return' to God who gave it?

The translation is correct as the original Hebrew reads:

וְהָרוּחַ תָּשׁוּב אֶל הָאֱלֹהִים אֲשֶׁר נְתָנָהּ ......(...ve ha ruach tashuv el ha elohim asher netanah). This literally means 'and the spirit returns to God who gave it.'

Let's review one more verse that supports pre-existence:

Will Not Leave Heaven Again?

Revelations 3:12 (NIV)

The one who is victorious I will make a pillar in the temple of my God. Never again will they leave it....

When not referring to our physical bodies, the temple of God is normally understood as Heaven. This verse is addressed to the church in ancient Philadelphia and promises that, if their spiritual strength is sufficient, they will go to Heaven and will never have to leave it again.

The Greek of the phrase in question reads: καὶ ἔξω οὐ μὴ ἐξέλθῃ ἔτι (kai exo ou me exelthe eti), and literally means 'and will not go out anymore.' So the word "again" in the verse should actually be 'anymore,' but the difference is negligible.

The main point is that without the word 'again' or 'anymore,' there would be nothing remarkable about this verse. The addition of this adverb, however, strongly implies that the people reading the verse were in Heaven before and left it at least once, presumably to incarnate at some point in the past.

Inevitable Questions about Pre-existence and Reincarnation?

I've seen several more verses that support the reality of pre-existence, but I think the ones we've reviewed will suffice. So let's now turn to a few questions that we inevitably raise regarding pre-existence and reincarnation:

Which Souls Incarnate?

An excellent question. Before we try to answer it, though, let's recall the different categories of souls that could possibly incarnate: 1) spirits or angels from Heaven, 2) souls from Hades/Sheol, 3) demons on earth.

By the way, if we were limiting souls from Hades/Sheol to just those from the Paradise region, we would not separate it from Heaven. As we know, Paradise and Heaven are virtually the same. But since we are including souls from both regions of the afterlife (Paradise and Tartarus), we have to separate them.

Demons Incarnate via Possession?

We could go on an on about demons, but it would be too time consuming, so we'll save that for another book. But the short answer about demons is that, yes, their incarnations are usually in the form of possession of a person who is already alive. And as we've already noted earlier in this book, many demons can possess or incarnate in a single person.

The Bible refers to demons as devils, unclean spirits, or impure spirits that need to be cast or driven out of people whom they possess:

Matthew 10:1 (NIV)

Jesus called his twelve disciples to him and gave them authority to drive out impure spirits and to heal every disease and sickness.

Matthew 17:18 (NIV)

Jesus rebuked the demon, and it came out of the boy, and he was healed at that moment.

Angels Incarnate for Special Missions?

Indeed they do. The Bible has numerous examples of angels incarnating in order to carry out special tasks among people, including the following two:

Acts 5:18, 19 (NIV)

They arrested the apostles and put them in the public jail. But during the night an angel of the Lord opened the prison doors and brought them out,...

Genesis 19:1-3, 15 (NIV)

The two angels arrived at Sodom in the evening, and Lot was sitting in the gateway of the city...He prepared a meal for them, baking bread without yeast, and they ate.

With the coming of dawn, the angels urged Lot, saying, "Hurry! Take your wife and your two daughters who are here, or you will be swept away when the city is punished."

As we can see in the two situations above, the angels came as flesh-and-blood people to carry out special missions, normally involving helping people in some way.

Souls From the Afterlife (Hades/Sheol) Incarnate for Entire Lifetimes?

I would assume that more souls from Sheol than from Heaven would incarnate for entire lifetimes, because those from Sheol would have more need to do so. This is because life on earth gives souls more opportunity to improve and develop spiritually. And we assume that souls from Hades need such opportunities more than those from Heaven.

So Souls Don't Have to Stay in the Afterlife (Hades/Sheol) Until Judgement Day?

Not necessarily. Yes, Sheol is generally the waiting area until Judgement Day. But no, souls do not necessarily remain there 100 percent of the time until then. As an analogy, if we're in the waiting room at a train station or an airport, must we wait there 100 percent of the time until the train or plane arrives?

No, we don't have to wait the entire time. As long as we return before boarding time, we can leave the waiting room for whatever special reason we have, whether it's to buy food, use the restroom, or something else.

By the same token, souls in Sheol may need to leave their waiting room for some reason, including the need to incarnate for some special purpose. For example, to learn a particular lesson or to develop spiritually more.

I'm sure souls don't just decide on a whim to leave the afterlife and incarnate, though. That would create a chaotic situation. Such decisions undoubtedly have to be planned and approved with some divine authority.

Do Pre-existence and Reincarnation Conflict at All with the Bible?

Not at all. Actually these concepts do the exact opposite—they make perfect sense of Bible teachings that seem unclear and reconcile Biblical teachings that seem to contradict reality.

For example, did it make sense when Jesus healed the paralyzed man by forgiving his past sins? No, not at first. But when we applied the concept that the man's past-life sins had caused his paralysis, it made perfect sense.

Regarding contradictions, for instance, the Bible tells us that whatever we do in life will have a corresponding effect on our future. The following verses illustrate this point:

Matthew 26:52 (NIV)

....Jesus said to him, "for all who draw the sword will die by the sword.

Galatians 6:7 (NIV)

Do not be deceived: God cannot be mocked. A man reaps what he sows.

Job 4:8 (NIV)

As I have observed, those who plow evil and those who sow trouble reap it.

These verses clearly say, again, that the things we do now will affect us in a corresponding manner in the future. But what if these effects don't happen during the same lifetime? For example, what if a man who gets rich by hurting and killing others actually has a very long, healthy, and enjoyable life? He certainly didn't reap what he sowed, right? So don't these verses contradict reality? Aren't they actually untrue in this man's case?

The Bible Is Only Correct If We Reincarnate?

Some of us might think that what this man reaps could be in the afterlife. However, these verses, especially Matthew 26:52, clearly indicate that what we reap will be in a physical life. After all, how can a spirit "die by the sword?"

So yes, those verses contradict reality; and yes, they are untrue—unless we look past this man's current life and into a future one. Then the contradiction disappears.

Another question we have undoubtedly asked ourselves is about how salvation fits into all of this. That, is can reincarnation be reconciled with salvation?

Can Reincarnation Be Reconciled with Salvation?

Absolutely! As a matter of fact, salvation and reincarnation fit together like hand in glove, and here's why:

An important similarity between Christianity and other major religions that teach reincarnation (like Hinduism and Buddhism) is that they all teach that we need to follow certain teachings and principles, including good works, to improve ourselves and develop spiritually until we achieve our goal of eternal life (Nirvana or Moksha for the Indian religions).

An important difference, however, is that, while those religions teach that one can enter Nirvana only by working to overcome negative *karma* in a long cycle of seemingly endless reincarnations, Christianity offers a much shorter path to Paradise and Heaven—salvation!

This means that God will allow us to either continue to "reap what we sow" through countless reincarnations until we become righteous enough for salvation and eternal life, or to accept His grace by simply repenting of our sins (negative karma) and receiving instant salvation through Jesus Christ!

This means that repenting for our sins and accepting Jesus Christ as our personal savior immediately triggers God's grace, which wipes away our sins and releases us from the law governing sins and, therefore, from the need for further incarnations:

Romans 6:14 (NIV)

For sin shall no longer be your master, because you are not under the law, but under grace.

Salvation releases us from the "law" of having to reincarnate until we overcome what we have sowed through our sins:

Revelations 3:12 (NKJV)

He who overcomes, I will make him a pillar in the temple of My God, and he shall go out no more.....

Since the temple of God in this verse is Heaven, and "overcomes" refers to overcoming sins and obtaining eternal life, "go out no more" must, therefore, mean that the overcomer, has 'gone out' of Heaven before. Could this mean anything other than the overcomer having multiple incarnations?

The original Greek of the main phrase here is καὶ ἔξω οὐ μὴ ἐξέλθῃ ἔτι (Kai exo ou me exelthe eti), which literally means 'and he will go out no more.'

So Do Those Who Spiritually "Overcome" Go Straight to Heaven?

In the chapter on post-mortem salvation, we learned that, after physical death, spiritually worthy souls immediately go to a part of the afterlife called Paradise that is essentially Heaven.

The Greatest Controversy of All?

Now that we have raised and answered the tough questions regarding our pre-existence and incarnations, we will address in our final chapter what many of us might believe is the greatest Biblical controversy of all, both in this book and the entire Bible—whether Jesus Christ and Melchizedek were spiritually the same!

CHAPTER XIX

Melchizedek and Jesus Christ -- Two of Many Divine Incarnations?

If God came down from Heaven to incarnate once as Jesus Christ, why could He not do it multiple times?

His mission as Jesus Christ was to bring salvation to the world as a faster way to overcome negative karma (sin). But what if God had incarnated for other missions for other purposes earlier? And what if one of those other missions was as Melchizedek? I think there is more than enough evidence showing precisely that.

To put it more plainly, the obvious connections and similarities between Melchizedek and Jesus Christ have led me to the conclusion that both men were incarnations of the same divine spirit. In other words, Melchizedek was an earlier incarnation of our Lord and Savior Jesus Christ.

Believe me, I didn't reach this conclusion overnight or easily. I had actually begun noticing the similarities years ago while reading Genesis 14 and Hebrews 7. Each time I read those chapters, however, I came away scratching my head, because I could not understand how or why a normal human being could be so similar to Jesus Christ.

A Biblical Puzzle Solved

This puzzle remained unsolved until I decided to open my mind to other possible sources of meaning and context outside of Genesis 14 and Hebrews 7. It worked. Those other sources pointed me towards a solution that brought all the pieces together to form a perfectly clear picture. A picture not only of those two incarnations of God, but also of several others.

Verses Supporting the Idea of Divine Incarnations on Earth?

To set the stage for the picture of Jesus' previous incarnation as Melchizedek, let's first see two verses that indicate that Jesus did indeed have earlier incarnations:

Micah 5:2 (NKJV)

But you, Bethlehem Ephrathah, though you are little among the thousands of Judah, Yet out of you shall come forth to Me The One to be Ruler in Israel, Whose goings forth are from of old, From everlasting."

We're certain of the translation, because the original Hebrew for "his goings forth" is ויתאצומ (motsitav), and it is derived from the basic three-letter verb אצי (yatsa), which literally means 'go out.'

Only One Person Fits the Description?

Micah prophesies here that a ruler from the tribe of Judah would be born in Bethlehem and that this ruler had been engaging in "goings forth" since very ancient times.

How many Biblical people can we think of who had lineage in the tribe of Judah, was born in Bethlehem, and was a type of ruler in

Israel? Well, as far as I know, Jesus is the only perfect match, because both Mary and Joseph had lineage in the tribe of Judah, Jesus was born in Bethlehem, and He was called 'King of the Jews' and 'King of Righteousness,' and he brought the Kingdom of Heaven to earth.

So, as far as I can see, Jesus was the only Biblical figure to fit the description of Micah's prophecy. And unless someone can think of another possible match, I would say the "goings forth" in this verse indicate that Jesus indeed had at least one earlier incarnation.

John 16: 28 (NKJV)

I came forth from the Father and have come into the world. Again, I leave the world and go to the Father."

Crystal Clear Evidence?

Indeed it is. This verse needs no interpretation at all because Jesus Christ Himself says that He was on earth previously:

I underlined the word 'again' so that the meaning and context is clear. Correct me if I'm wrong, but, in order to leave the world 'again,' wouldn't He have to have been here before?

NIV Omitted the Original Greek Word for 'Again'

By the way, I used the NKJ version for this verse because NIV, for whatever reason, omitted the original Greek word for 'again':

Πάλιν ἀφίημι τὸν κόσμον…(Palin afiemi ton kosmon…) This literally means 'again I leave the world…' The Greek word for 'again' is underlined.

Two Ways to Give the Same Message?

Essentially yes. To briefly review these two verses, one is a prophetic message that Jesus would again leave Heaven to return to earth, while the second is a statement by Jesus Himself that He would again leave earth to return to Heaven. Either way the result is the same, right?

What about Specific Divine Incarnations?

Besides Melchizedek and Jesus, does the Bible tell of any other specific incarnations of God? Absolutely. And here are three of them that are virtually irrefutable (especially number three):

Genesis 3:8 (NIV)

Then the man and his wife heard the sound of the LORD God as he was walking in the in the cool of the day, and they hid from the LORD God among the trees of the garden.

I'm pretty sure that most of us, including myself, have read the details of this divine encounter in the Garden of Eden without thinking of it in terms of a divine incarnation. But if we focus for a moment on exactly what happened there, we might see it differently.

As a quick background reminder, let's recall that God was already personally interacting with Adam and Eve after creating them. For example, He communicated directly with them on things like their role among the various life forms on earth and what to eat from the trees in the Garden of Eden.

God Was an Actual Person in the Garden of Eden?

Yes. Many of us were probably thinking that Adam and Eve could perhaps just hear God's voice, but not actually see Him as a person. But Genesis 3:8 indicates that He was indeed a person. It says that God was "walking" in the Garden. Unless my memory fails me, in order to walk, we need legs. Physical legs. But was God just a pair of legs with no upper body? I think not. So God was in the Garden of Eden with Adam and Eve in a complete body.

Is there any other confirmation that God was there in the flesh? Yes there is. First, this verse tells us that Adam and Eve "heard the sound" of God walking. Second, they "hid" from Him. But could they try to hide from God without first knowing where He was-- physically? And how could they know that unless they could also see Him--physically?

So there is no way God could have interacted with Adam and Eve and the physical environment around them in the manner that He did unless He was there in the flesh. In other words, unless He had temporarily incarnated for that purpose.

And, by the way, while interacting with Adam and Eve, God was identified as יְהֹוָה (Yehovah), whom we normally think of as Jehovah or Yahweh. Although some Bible scholars say Yahweh is the entire Trinity, other scholars point to many verses in the Bible (like those in Psalm 110) that say that Yahweh is only God the Father. Either way, however, it was definitely God who incarnated in the Garden of Eden.

Even Clearer Evidence of a Divine Incarnation?

Yes, Genesis 32 shows even clearer evidence that God appeared in the flesh. Remember the story of Jacob wresting with the "Angel?":

I. Genesis 32: 24-30 (NIV)

24 So Jacob was left alone, and a man wrestled with him till daybreak.

25 When the man saw that he could not overpower him, he touched the socket of Jacob's hip so that his hip was wrenched as he wrestled with the man.

26 Then the man said, "Let me go, for it is daybreak."

But Jacob replied, "I will not let you go unless you bless me."

27 The man asked him, "What is your name? "Jacob," he answered.

28 Then the man said, "Your name will no longer be Jacob, but Israel, because you have struggled with God and with humans and have overcome."

29 Jacob said, "Please tell me your name." But he replied, "Why do you ask my name?" Then he blessed him there.

30 So Jacob called the place Peniel, saying, "It is because I saw God face to face, and yet my life was spared."

What These Verses Mean

Some of us will undoubtedly ask: Wasn't this mysterious man an angel? The answer is no, He was not an angel. The following facts tell why:

Jacob was convinced that the stranger was God, and asked for His blessings.

The stranger blessed him and changed his name to Israel.

The stranger told Jacob that he had now struggled with both God and men and prevailed.

Jacob named that location Peniel (פניאל) in verse 30, which literally means 'the face of God'

Not an Angel?

No. It was God Himself. But why would God Himself come to Jacob instead of sending an angel? Let's recall from the previous chapter that divine beings would sometimes incarnate temporarily for special purposes or missions that lasted for only a short time.

Sometimes they were angels who incarnated, but in certain more important situations, they were God. For example, for the creation of humans and instructing them in the Garden of Eden, it was God. For bringing salvation to mankind, it was God.

So it stands to reason that to prepare for the creation of the twelve tribes of His chosen people, it would also be God. In this case, Jacob, after his physical encounter with God, becomes the father and grandfather of those tribes.

The Clearest Evidence of All that God Incarnated on Earth?

Genesis 18 might contain the clearest and most indisputable evidence that we've seen of a divine incarnation other than Jesus, as this chapter recounts God's visit to Abraham where He demonstrates His omnipotence in two astounding ways:

III. Genesis 18: 1, 2, 13, 14, 17-19, 25, 26 (NIV)

The Lord appeared to Abraham near the great trees of Mamre while he was sitting at the entrance to his tent in the heat of the day.

2 Abraham looked up and saw three men standing nearby. When he saw them, he hurried from the entrance of his tent to meet them and bowed low to the ground.

13 Then the Lord said to Abraham, "Why did Sarah laugh and say, 'Will I really have a child, now that I am old?'

14 Is anything too hard for the Lord? I will return to you at the appointed time next year, and Sarah will have a son."

17 Then the Lord said, "Shall I hide from Abraham what I am about to do?

18 Abraham will surely become a great and powerful nation, and all nations on earth will be blessed through him.

19 For I have chosen him, so that he will direct his children and his household after him to keep the way of the Lord by doing what is right and just, so that the Lord will bring about for Abraham what he has promised him."

25 Far be it from you to do such a thing—to kill the righteous with the wicked, treating the righteous and the wicked alike. Far be it from you! Will not the Judge of all the earth do right?"

26 The Lord said, "If I find fifty righteous people in the city of Sodom, I will spare the whole place for their sake."

An Astounding Visit by God Himself!

These verses are without a doubt the most explicit evidence of divine pre-Jesus incarnations that we've seen thus far. And here's why:

- *Jehovah* (aka *Yahweh*) is specifically named as one of the three visitors! Although NIV and most other versions refer to Him as "the Lord" throughout the chapter, the original Hebrew verses call Him יְהוָֹה (Yehovah), which, as most of us know, is *Jehovah*.
- The first two verses say that God appeared in the form of a man along with two other beings who looked like men, and all three were standing near Abraham.
- In Verses 13 and 14, God causes Sarah, who is way beyond childbearing age, to have a baby at age 90.
- In verses 18 and 19, God chooses Abraham as the patriarch of a new nation of chosen people.
- In verse 25, Abraham calls God the judge of all the earth.
- In verse 26, God is about to destroy Sodom.

- No angel could have done these things and certainly would not have been called *Jehovah* or the "judge of all the earth." It was clearly God Himself.

Now Jesus and Melchizedek?

Yes, we're finally there. After seeing Biblical evidence of other divine incarnations, let's finally focus on the main one in this chapter—Jesus' previous incarnation as Melchizedek.

For the rest of this chapter, we'll examine very strong evidence from multiple Biblical sources that Melchizedek and Jesus Christ were two incarnations of the same spirit:

Earliest Biblical Evidence

The Bible's first mention of Melchizedek occurred in Genesis 14. Abraham had just returned from a successful battle to free his nephew Lot from his captives, and Melchizedek walked out to meet him:

Genesis 14: 18-20 (NIV)

Then Melchizedek king of Salem brought out bread and wine. He was priest of God Most High, and he blessed Abram, saying, "Blessed be Abram by God Most High, Creator of heaven and earth.

And praise be to God Most High, who delivered your enemies into your hand." Then Abram gave him a tenth of everything.

Compelling Parallels Between Melchizedek and Jesus

Melchizedek was the King of Righteousness

Melchizedek is a Hebrew name--מַלְכִּי־צֶדֶק (malki-tsedek) that literally means *king* or *ruler of righteousness.*

Jesus, of course, was the *King of Righteousness* throughout the entire New Testament and prophetic areas of the Old Testament. For example, a verse that also reaffirms Jesus' lineage from King David, includes a prophecy to David about his descendent Jesus' righteousness and kingdom:

> Jeremiah 23:5 (ESV): *"Behold, the days are coming, declares the LORD, when I will raise up for David a righteous Branch, and he shall reign as king and deal wisely, and shall execute justice and righteousness in the land.*

By the way, I didn't use the NIV translation here, because it completely omitted the Hebrew word for righteousness, which is הַקְדָצ (tsedakah).

Melchizedek Was also the King of Peace

In addition to being the earlier name for Jerusalem, *Salem* is related to the Hebrew word for peace. So, since Melchizedek was the king of Salem, it means He was the *king of peace.*

Jesus was called *ruler of peace* in Isaiah 9:6 (NIV):

> *For to us a child is born, to us a son is given, and the government will be on his shoulders. And he will be called Wonderful Counselor, Mighty God, Everlasting Father, Prince of Peace.*

Salem was the city that was later called *Jerusalem*.

Jerusalem, of course, was the capital of the land of God's (and therefore Jesus') chosen people.

How can we be sure Salem and Jerusalem were the same? Well, Psalm 76:2 (NIV) says it is: *His tent is in Salem, his dwelling place in Zion.*

As some of us probably know, *Zion* is another Biblical word for Jerusalem.

Melchizedek gave Abraham *bread and wine*.

As most of us surely recall, at the last supper, Jesus stressed the sacramental importance of bread and wine by equating His own body with bread and His own blood with wine.

Translation Problem

Note that the end of the verse above says "Prince of Peace" and not ruler. Unfortunately, NIV and several other versions translate the original Hebrew שַׂר שָׁלוֹם (sar shalom) as "Prince of Peace," which is incorrect. The literal translation is closer to 'ruler of peace,' however, because the meaning of שַׂר (sar) is someone who rules, leads, or governs, like a ruler. In certain limited contexts, *sar* could have meant prince. But in this context, it definitely means *ruler* or some other primary leader, not a second-in-command like a prince.

We can verify this with another Hebrew word that appears in the very same verse. This is the word for "government," which is הַמִּשְׂרָה (misrah). This word contains the word *sar* (ruler): Note the 'sr' in the middle of 'misrah.' This is the רשׂ (sar) or 'ruler' that we're discussing.

So it's no coincidence that two almost identical words appear in one verse. It clearly means they belong together contextually.

In addition, someone who leads a government today would be called a prime minister or president, but in Biblical times they were called rulers, not princes. Hebrew has a couple of words more commonly used for prince. One is נָסִיךְ (nasich) and the other is מֶלֶךְ בֶּן (ben melech), which literally means 'king's son.'

The Kicker

As a kicker for our point, Kings 20:14 is a verse that contains the very same word רַשׂ (sar) in a plural (and genitive) form. And that is שָׂרֵי (sarei). NIV and other versions translate the singular form as "prince," so, for consistency, they should translate the plural as 'princes,' right? Yes, but they don't. Not even close. They actually translated the plural form correctly with words like 'leaders,' 'governors,' and 'commanders.' So it seems that some translations value style over accuracy.

More Parallels Between Melchizedek and Jesus in Hebrews 7

As we're about to see, Hebrews 7 has several more parallels between Melchizedek and Jesus that make their spiritual connection even clearer:

> **Hebrews 7** (NIV):
>
> *This Melchizedek was king of Salem and priest of God Most High. He met Abraham returning from the defeat of the kings and blessed him,*

2 and Abraham gave him a tenth of everything. First, the name Melchizedek means "king of righteousness"; then also, "king of Salem" means "king of peace."

Without father or mother, without genealogy, without beginning of days or end of life, resembling the Son of God, he remains a priest forever.

4 Just think how great he was: Even the patriarch Abraham gave him a tenth of the plunder!

Now the law requires the descendants of Levi who become priests to collect a tenth from the people— that is, from their fellow Israelites—even though they also are descended from Abraham.

6 This man, however, did not trace his descent from Levi, yet he collected a tenth from Abraham and blessed him who had the promises.

And without doubt the lesser is blessed by the greater.

8 In the one case, the tenth is collected by people who die; but in the other case, by him who is declared to be living.

One might even say that Levi, who collects the tenth, paid the tenth through Abraham,

10 because when Melchizedek met Abraham, Levi was still in the body of his ancestor.

If perfection could have been attained through the Levitical priesthood—and indeed the law given to the people established that priesthood—why was there still need for another priest to come, one in the order of Melchizedek, not in the order of Aaron?

12 For when the priesthood is changed, the law must be changed also.

He of whom these things are said belonged to a different tribe, and no one from that tribe has ever served at the altar.

14 For it is clear that our Lord descended from Judah, and in regard to that tribe Moses said nothing about priests.

And what we have said is even more clear if another priest like Melchizedek appears,

16 one who has become a priest not on the basis of a regulation as to his ancestry but on the basis of the power of an indestructible life.

For it is declared: "You are a priest forever, in the order of Melchizedek."

18 The former regulation is set aside because it was weak and useless

(for the law made nothing perfect), and a better hope is introduced, by which we draw near to God.

20 And it was not without an oath! Others became priests without any oath, but he became a priest with an oath when God said to him: "The Lord has sworn and will not change his mind: 'You are a priest forever.'"

22 Because of this oath, Jesus has become the guarantor of a better covenant.

Now there have been many of those priests, since death prevented them from continuing in office;

24 but because Jesus lives forever, he has a permanent priesthood.

Therefore he is able to save completely those who come to God through him, because he always lives to intercede for them.

26 Such a high priest truly meets our need—one who is holy, blameless, pure, set apart from sinners, exalted above the heavens.

Unlike the other high priests, he does not need to offer sacrifices day after day, first for his own sins, and then for the sins of the people. He sacrificed for their sins once for all when he offered himself.

28 For the law appoints as high priests men in all their weakness; but the oath, which came after the law, appointed the Son, who has been made perfect forever.

What These Verses Tell Us

Here's what we learned from Hebrews 7 (we'll only include relevant verses, and we won't repeat points from Genesis 14):

Abraham Gave Tithes To Melchizedek

The fact that Abraham tithed to Melchizedek is remarkable in two ways. First, this is the very first recorded instance of anyone tithing to anyone anywhere in the Bible, as it preceded the traditional tithing that started after the establishment of the Hebrew Levitical priesthood by Aaron.

Second, the fact that the very first recorded tithes were offered to Melchizedek means that Abraham elevated Melchizedek to a level far above himself and anyone else he knew and acknowledged him as someone with a very special relationship with God. That relationship was, of course, that Melchizedek was actually part of God.

Both Jesus And Melchizedek Were Born and Lived Under Miraculous Circumstances

Their Miraculous Birth: Jesus was born through divine impregnation of Mary, meaning He had no biological father. Melchizedek, even more miraculously, had neither biological father nor mother. No recorded genealogy at all!

Melchizedek's Miraculous Existence: Again, no evidence existed that Melchizedek was ever born or that he ever died biologically. This strongly indicates that, since he did not have a mission of salvation like his later incarnation Jesus had, he did not have to interact with people to the personal extent that Jesus did, and so there was no need for Melchizedek to go through the "normal" biological birth-to-death process that humans go through. The bottom line is that his very existence, for as long as he walked the earth, was a miracle.

Jesus' Miraculous Life: In addition to being divinely conceived and born, Jesus' life was replete with miracles. For example: He cast out demons (Mark 5), healed a paralyzed man (John 5), walked on water (John 6), and raised Lazarus from the dead (John 11), among other miracles.

Jesus and Melchizedek's Were Equals

Jesus' priesthood was modeled after Melchizedek's

Melchizedek set the standard during His lifetime that Jesus later attained during His. This is made even clearer by verse 17 (NIV) that says that Jesus was *"...a priest forever, in the order of Melchizedek."*

The Greek word that NIV and most other versions translate as "order" is τάξιν (taksin) from the basic word τάξις (taxis), and "order" is one of the possible translations of τάξις.

'Type,' not 'order': But what does the "order" in verse 17 mean? The word 'order' could mean several things, depending on the context, including an arrangement, a position, rank, group, society (Masonic order, fraternal order of police, religious order, etc). So just using 'order' is unclear, to say the least.

In addition to the above-mentioned possibilities, the Greek word τάξις (taxis) also means kind or type. This translation fits contextually and makes more sense than the nebulous word 'order.'

So when we read Hebrews 7:17, we should understand that it means that Jesus' priesthood was not the same "order," but the same exact type as Melchizedek's. In other words, equal to Melchizedek's.

This and the fact that Jesus and Melchizedek were the only two priests of this type to ever live on earth is further evidence that the two are incarnations of the same spirit.

Both Melchizedek and Christ possessed "indestructible life": According to verse 16, their priesthood is based not on ancestry, as the Levitical priesthood was, but on the "power of an indestructible life."

Recalling that Melchizedek was without beginning of days or end of life (Hebrews 7:3 NIV), that "Jesus lives forever...," (Hebrews 7:24 NIV), and that both are "…priests forever…," we clearly see that they have the "power of an indestructible life."

Melchizedek Was Made Like the Son of God

Let's just focus for a while on this heading. It says Melchizedek was made like the Son of God. And since Jesus is the Son of God, it unmistakably means that Melchizedek was made to be like Jesus. So far, we've been discovering that Melchizedek and Jesus were alike by reading about all the similarities between them, but Hebrews 7:3 actually tells us in very clear terms that Melchizedek was not only similar to Jesus, but that he was made to be like Him.

Only Person in the Bible to Be Compared to Jesus Christ: Melchizedek is the only person in the entire Bible to be compared to Jesus in terms of having similar qualities. This is obviously very compelling evidence that Melchizedek, in fact, became Jesus.

NIV Mistranslation: Although the NIV translation of Hebrews 7:3 above says Melchizedek was "resembling" the Son of God, the word 'resembling' here is unfortunately another NIV mistranslation. The Greek word that NIV mistranslated is ἀφωμοιωμένος (afomoiomenos), which means 'having been made like.' And that is very different from simply 'resembling.'

So Hebrews 7:3 should read: "…, having been made like the Son of God, he remains a priest forever."

The Correct Translation Changes the Meaning?

Does the correct translation change the meaning? You bet it does. The most important thing to note is that the correct translation tells us that the strong similarities between Jesus and Melchizedek were not coincidental, they didn't just happen. It was by design. That is, they were the result of a deliberate divine plan to give Melchizedek and Jesus virtually the same qualities.

In other words, God the Father intentionally planned to incarnate God the Son as Melchizedek and then to reincarnate Him later as Jesus Christ.

King David Confirms Jesus' Divine Connection to Melchizedek

In one of his psalms, King David celebrated the fact that God had elevated Jesus Christ to the priesthood rank of Melchizedek.

What makes this psalm even more interesting is that King David is actually addressing Jesus Christ about what God the Father had done for Him vis-à-vis the priesthood. Note the fact that David calls both of them "Lord" in verse 1:

Psalm 110: 1, 4 (NIV):

The Lord says to my lord:"Sit at my right hand..."

It's interesting but confusing that NIV and a few other versions translate both God the Father and God the Son as "Lord" in the first verse.

Confusing Translation of 'Yahweh'

Calling both God the Father and God the Son 'Lord' confuses the reader, because we don't know which one is meant.

Checking the original Hebrew for verse 1, we see לאדני שב לימיני נאום יהוה (neum Yehovah laAdoni shev liyemini), which actually means 'Jehovah (Yahweh) says to my Lord (Jesus), "Sit at my right hand…"'

So the original Hebrew tells us explicitly which parts of the Trinity are involved by pointing out which is the Father and which is the Son. This is much clearer than simply saying "The Lord says to my Lord."

Verse 4

Then in verse 4, which is the main verse for our point, "Lord" is used only once, and by context we know that it refers to God the Father. So what David does in verse 4 is that he addresses Jesus directly and comments that Jehovah had sworn to make Jesus a priest forever of the same type as Melchizedek:

> *The Lord has sworn and will not change his mind:*
> *"You are a priest forever in the order of Melchizedek."*

So we have Biblical witnesses of the equality of Jesus and Melchizedek not only in Genesis 14 and Hebrews 7, but also Psalms 110.

The Kicker That Re-confirms Jesus' Previous Life as Melchizedek

After researching and accumulating tons of Biblical evidence that Jesus had lived at least one prior incarnation on earth and that he had incarnated as Melchizedek, I had an itchy feeling that something was still missing.

But with so much evidence that Jesus had lived as Melchizedek, what could be missing? What else could we possibly need for a puzzle that was already complete?

The Glue that Strengthens the Puzzle?

Exactly. Those of us who love putting together picture puzzles probably recall that after we finish putting the pieces together, we still need to put a coat of glue on it, right?

Well, the glue that I thought we still needed was confirmation from Jesus Himself that he had previously incarnated as Melchizedek. We've seen a staggering amount of evidence that He did, but none where He Himself said that He did. So did He ever actually say that He had lived as Melchizedek?

He absolutely did. In John Chapter 8:

The Re-confirmation

To very briefly explain the context of the following verses, Pharisees were challenging Jesus' statements about His divine origin. Then, after Jesus told them that they would never die if they obeyed His word, they argued that if their "father" Abraham had to die, then no one, including Jesus, could have power over death. And then Jesus replied as follows:

John 8:56-58 (ESV)

Your father Abraham rejoiced that he would see my day. He saw it and was glad."

So the Jews said to him, "You are not yet fifty years old, and have you seen Abraham?"

Jesus said to them, "Truly, truly, I say to you, before Abraham was, I am."

A Slight Translation Issue

For those of us who noticed that we're using the English Standard version of these verses instead of NIV, the reason is that the NIV translation says "….at the thought of seeing my day," while the original Greek—ἵνα ἴδῃ τὴν ἡμέραν τὴν ἐμήν (hina ide ten hemeran ten even)—literally means '…that he would see my day.'

What These Verses Tell Us

"Day" is an earthly unit of time: When Jesus said that Abraham saw His "day" and was "glad," what did He mean by His "day?" The Greek word for "day" in this verse is ἡμέρα (hemera), and it refers to 'day' in the sense of a literal unit of time as measured by people on earth. That is, the word refers to either a 24-hour period of time or a longer, but still limited period of time. In this verse, it probably means the latter.

Three other reasons why we know that "day" means a literal unit of time on earth are:

- All mentions of time in the Bible refer in some way to earth-related issues.
- The Bible tells us that time is not measured in the spirit world (Psalm 90:4, John 8:58, 2 Peter 3:8…).
- The "day" referred to in these verses was the particular (earthly) time period when Abraham was alive.

Jesus was incarnated on earth: The fact that Jesus subjected Himself to a limited period of earthly time ("my day") meant that He was on earth and in an earthly body at the time because, again, spirits cannot be subjected to or limited by time and, therefore, cannot have "days."

Jesus met Abraham as Melchizedek: So, since Jesus told us very clearly that He had encountered Abraham in the past, and since we now know that He was in a physical body at the time, who else could He have been if not Melchizedek? The fact that this encounter made Abraham happy was certainly consistent with his tithing to Melchizedek and sharing bread and wine with him.

Jesus' encounter with Abraham while incarnated as Melchizedek, therefore, dovetails perfectly with the abundance of evidence we have seen that Jesus and Melchizedek shared the same spirit.

CHAPTER SUMMARY

In a nutshell, our discussion in this chapter began and developed from one simple question: If we accept the fact that God incarnated once in the physical body of the human named Jesus at one particular time and for one particular mission on earth, why then could we not accept the idea that God incarnated in the physical body of other humans at other times for other missions on earth?

We then reviewed many Bible verses, stories, principles, and facts that, when combined contextually, form a very clear and coherent picture of multiple divine incarnations throughout history, with the main incarnations being Melchizedek and Jesus. From the same Biblical sources, we were also able to see at least partial pictures of God's missions during these incarnations.

After seeing abundant Biblical evidence that God has indeed incarnated many times on earth, including Melchizedek's later incarnation as Jesus Christ, we repeated the chapter's first question, hoping that so much evidence from the Bible itself would make it easier for us to let go of the old assumption that God incarnated only once.

Finally, regarding Melchizedek's mission, even though we don't have a lot of Biblical details, we do know that it had to involve some aspect of his eternal priesthood. After all, from what we can gather from the Bible, Melchizedek's priesthood was his most important quality, especially since it was a quality shared by only one other entity in all of existence—our Lord and Savior Jesus Christ!

AFTERWORD

To those of us who may be wondering why I wrote a book on such controversial topics, my main purpose was simply to share questions that I had posed and answers that I had found regarding interesting topics that happened to also be controversial.

My hope while writing this book was that any answers that emerged would shed a little more clarity not only on the topics themselves, but also on our need to grow in the most important area in mankind's past, present, and future—our spirituality.

If I had to list the most important points resulting from my research and prayers while writing this book, I would say the following:

We are primarily spiritual beings that leave eternity to experience brief incarnations on earth. So our times on earth are extremely short stopovers on our journey homeward. (James 4:14, Psalm 39: 4-5)

God is our spiritual Father. We should strive to love Him above all else and to return to Him as quickly as possible through the salvation offered through our Lord and Savior Jesus Christ. (John 14: 6, John 3:16)

We are all spiritual brothers and sisters, regardless of external differences (Romans 12: 5, Galatians 3: 28). We should therefore love others as siblings and as ourselves (1 John 4: 7, 20, Romans 12: 10).

We must bear in mind that love is the key to spiritual development and that God's most important quality is love (1 John 4: 8). We should therefore strive to continually increase our love for God and for other people (Mark 12: 30, 31).

ILLUSTRATIONS

Cover Image: Jeronym Pilikovsky, pixabay.com

1.1: Bible: pixabay.com

2.1: Light: pixabay.com

3.1: Sky: pixabay.com

3.2: Light at end of tunnel: pixabay.com

4.1: Gates: pixabay.com

4.2: Hellish creature, pixabay.com

5.1: Light, pixabay.com

6.1: Holding Jesus' hand, pixabay.com

7.1: Ocean waves: pixabay.com

8.1: Angel figure: pixabay.com

9.1: Fire: pixabay.com

10.1: Two hands: pixabay.com

11.1: Cross: pixabay.com

12.1: Crucifix: pixabay.com

13.1: Crowd: pixabay.com

13.2: Souls in Purgatory: picryl.com

14.1: Hellfire: Patheos.com

14.2: Valley of Hinnom: picryl.com

15.1: Heaven and Hell, pixabay.com

15.2: Purgatory, pixabay.com

16.1: Sky and crowd: pixabay.com

17.1: Woman leading prayer: pixabay.com

18.1. Three faces, pixabay.com

19.1 Crowd of faces: pixabay.com

Printed in the United States
by Baker & Taylor Publisher Services